Topline, Bottom Line:
A Simple, Brief, Comprehensive, and Irreverent Writing Guide for Professionals

by
Robert Levine

ISBN: 978-1-387-31424-9

To all my co-workers, past and present

Acknowledgements

Most of the material in this book was originally published serially on www.helium.com.

TABLE OF CONTENTS

PART 1: ELEMENTS OF WRITING

PART 2: TYPES OF PROFESSIONAL WRITING

Part 1: Elements of Writing

INTRODUCTION

Mark my words: someday soon, writers will rule the world.

I know that statement sounds outlandish, but I have my reasons for making it. We are in the later stages of shifting from an industrial economy to a service economy—just as, some 200 years ago, we shifted from an agricultural and artisan economy to an industrial one. One of the most highly demanded services in the business world today is providing information, whether commercial, demographic, scientific, technical, legal, scholarly, or any other type; we all know that we are well into the Information Age, thanks to the personal computer, e-mail, the Internet, the fax, and other technologies. For information to be of any use, however, it must be communicated as clearly and precisely as possible. Professionals who do not understand this fact will likely go the way of those late Eighteenth Century weavers who tried to compete with the new industrial textile factories.

Unfortunately, I have encountered too many professionals who do not understand the importance of effective communication, or at least are incapable of it. This holds true especially for writing. In my short but varied working life, I have seen college graduates, some with advanced degrees, make mistakes in writing that no native English-speaker intelligent enough to land a white-collar job should: using wrong homonyms (*there* or *they're* instead of *their*), misusing words, writing compound words as two separate words instead of writing them as a single or hyphenated word, typing a hyphen in place of a dash, betraying complete ignorance of the semicolon, and occasionally failing to recognize incomplete sentences. A great number of the professionals I have worked with clearly do not prioritize writing within their individual skills sets.

Education is an obvious culprit in this sad state of affairs. Too often, the rules of language are taught in isolation from their practical use, and as writing teacher Michael Degen states in *Crafting Expository Argument*, "Research demonstrates that teaching grammar without applying it to writing assignments does not improve student writing, but the teaching of writing with simultaneous instruction in the specifics of grammar usage and sentence structure will produce writers skillful in using language." If the rules of language are taught at all, that is. Lynne Truss, in her bestselling *Eats, Shoots and Leaves*, relates:

> There was a comical moment in the fifth year when our English teacher demanded, "But you *have* had lessons in grammar?" and we all looked shifty, as if the fault was ours. We had been taught Latin, French and German grammar; but English grammar was something we felt we were expected to infer from our reading ...

Although Truss skewers the British school system here, I can vouch that similar problems exist in American schools. One day in my high school French class, my poor teacher had to put the better part of a grammar lesson on hold because she first needed to explain to a number of students what direct and indirect objects were—not only the difference between them, but what they were. I had learned that in my English classes in middle school, or maybe even the upper grades of elementary school, mainly through the sadistic hazing rite known as diagramming sentences. Most of my grammatically deprived classmates in high school French were a year or two behind me; I may have been among the last American students to be taught sentence diagrams. Apparently, school systems on both sides of the Atlantic fail to grasp that, as Degen writes,

> when students leave the classroom, they will be asked in almost any profession to write exposition, to move from data to conclusion with clarity and sophistication. Throughout students' lives they will be frequently asked to draw conclusions from facts, to reorder information, to argue from information, to explain and to describe, whether they be preparing a legal brief, an argument to an insurance company to pay for medical treatment, a proposal to corporate executives, or a computer instruction manual.

As for myself, I can only echo Lynne Truss: "Luckily, I was exceptionally interested in English and got there in the end."

Another favorite place to point to in explaining the low quality of many professionals' writing is, paradoxically, one of the main reasons I mentioned why good writing should be so important for professionals: the Internet and e-mail. Lynne Truss explains, "In the 1970s"— when, according to her, British writing pedagogy was at its nadir—"no educationist could have predicted the explosion in universal written communication caused by the personal computer, the internet and the key pad of the mobile phone." Never mind that Truss uses the clumsy "educationist" over the more standard *educator* and doesn't capitalize the first letter in *Internet*. Her point, obviously on the mark, is that recent technologies allow businesses and organizations to procure and disseminate much more information than could be imagined in decades past. Nonetheless, while increasing the feasible volume of communication, they have not inspired quality in the communication delivered through them. Mainly, their very nature prevents this from happening. Truss contrasts the Internet with print media:

> The printed word is presented to us in a linear way, with syntax supreme in conveying the sense of the words in their order.... The book remains static and fixed; the reader journeys through it.... Knowing that the printed word is always edited, typeset and proofread before it reaches us, we appreciate its literary authority. Having paid money for it (often), we have a sense of investment ...
> All these conditions for reading are overturned by the new technologies. Information is presented to us in a non-linear way, through an exponential series of lateral associations. The internet is a public "space" which you visit, and even inhabit; its product is inherently impersonal and disembodied. Scrolling documents is the opposite of reading: your eyes remain static, while the material flows past.... Electronic media are intrinsically ephemeral.... the material on the internet is unmediated, except by the technology itself. And having no price, it has questionable value.

Her argument equally applies to conditions for writing. In the Paleolithic Era, when the post office monopolized the delivery of written correspondence, people had a tactile relationship with the letters and documents they wrote. They held the pen that wrote the words or punched the keys that struck them onto the paper. They folded the paper, inserted it into the envelope, sealed the envelope, and mailed it by hand. The recipient opened it by hand, unfolded the paper, and saw evidence of the writer's physical contact with the letter or document in his or her handwriting or in the type. Because senders' and recipients' bodies were more involved in the writing, the sender, at least subconsciously, felt that he or she put more of himself or herself into the writing, and felt driven by self-respect to make it as presentable as possible.

Also, the restriction to hard copy meant that different kinds of correspondence or documents could be written in different ways. When writing a personal letter by hand, the soft scratching of the pen's point on the paper whispered to the writer that he or she was among friends and need not fuss over the technicalities of formal language; the firmness of the keys, the snap of the type hitting the page, and the rigid return of the carriage when typing a business letter or professional document set the writer in the frame of mind to adhere strictly to the standards of written prose. With e-mail, where the computer keys emit the same hushed tap and the screen displays the same mix of light and shadow for both types of communication, nothing in the act of writing fosters any distinction in tone or mood between them in the writer's mind.

As a result, the ephemerality that Lynne Truss refers to seduces many people into approaching their writing more casually than they should. They feel that since their writing only exists—or, at least, was only intended to exist—in pixels and cyberspace rather than in ink and paper, it doesn't count as much as if it were published in a print venue. Lynne Truss quotes a movie review on Amazon.com that contained 11 (by my count) errors in its first paragraph.

Employers have been quick to seize on the benefits of information and communication technologies but slow to understand this drawback. Truss mentions a "*Washington Post* news story [that] explained the benefits of emailing: it 'increased employees' productivity by 1.8 hours a day *because they took less time to formulate their thoughts*.'" I have a feeling, though, that this increase in productivity offsets its own contribution to the bottom line: when writers take less time to formulate their thoughts, their audiences usually end up taking more time to decipher them.

Another common reason for faulty writing among professionals exists, which many commentators overlook: they don't care. They know their writing isn't Pulitzer Prize material, but they're businesspeople—they studied management, marketing, finance, accounting, statistics, computer science, or law, not English. As long as their clients haven't complained about their writing, who cares?

YOU should care, if you are professional. First, call me a fascist, but standards exist for a reason. Writing has "rules" for the same reason football and baseball do: they define and reinforce the goal of the activity and allow everyone involved to know what to expect so everything can go more smoothly. As Bill Bryson writes in *Bryson's Dictionary of Troublesome Words*,

> Just as we all agree that clarity is better served if *cup* represents a drinking vessel and *cap* something you put on your head, so too, I would submit, the world is a fractionally better place if we agree to preserve a distinction between *its* and *it's*, between "I lay down the law" and "I lie down to sleep," between *imply* and *infer*, *forego* and *forgo*, *flout* and *flaunt*, *anticipate* and *expect*, and countless others.

Your clients certainly expect you to preserve these distinctions. They want their money's worth. Diana Roberts Wienbroer, Elaine Hughes, and Jay Silverman warn in *Rules of Thumb for Business Writers*: "... remember that your writing reflects on you; errors, even in an e-mail, indicate to some readers that you don't care enough—that you do not bother to get details right."

Business writing is about saving face—or better, keeping it—so "recognize that basic errors in writing can cost you prestige, time—and even money." That's why when we're hiring people for my project and I receive résumés or cover letters with grammatical or typographical errors, that use words that don't make sense in context or don't even exist, I instantly delete them from my e-mail; if the person can't communicate carefully and articulately in applying for the job, he or she won't be able to on the job. And don't let the apparent ephemerality of e-mail and the Internet deceive you into thinking that what you write there is disposable. Even if you edit website content that changes periodically, your clients or bosses can always print out the originals and hold onto them—and hold them against you.

Recall that Amazon movie review cited in *Eats, Shoots and Leaves*. Would you accept the opinion of someone guilty of so many mistakes in his or her writing as authoritative? An artist neighbor of mine when I was growing up once said that thought means nothing without expression; if someone cannot properly articulate his or her thoughts, it's likely that he or she has not adequately formed those thoughts. "In fact," *The New St. Martin's Handbook* observes,

> research shows that writing encourages and enhances certain kinds of learning and even that some kinds of complex thinking are extremely difficult to sustain without it. Writing, then, is not a mysterious artistic talent that only a lucky few are born with but an essential and powerful means of discovering what you know and communicating that knowledge to others.

Thus, if professionals don't bone up on their writing skills, I see only one possible outcome: writers will dominate the new information-driven economy. Professionals will be at writers' mercy to transact any business, making writers a privileged class—the new technocrats. After having been economically marginalized and financially desperate for so long, some writers will likely abuse their position of power, perhaps to the point of extortion.

Although I'm a writer myself, for some reason, this future doesn't sit well with me. I guess I'm one of those antiquated classical humanists who still believes in the "well-rounded" person. We should all possess a little basic knowledge and skill in each major field of human endeavor; we shouldn't have to depend on specialists for everything outside of our own specialties. Maybe I'm a traitor to my vocation, but I believe that people other than trained career writers can master the fundamentals of writing well. So I'm going to help.

Who am I, you may ask, to presume such an undertaking? I majored in English at the University of Maryland, where I studied Advanced Composition and tutored fellow students in the campus writing center. Then I received a Master of Fine Arts degree in creative writing at Emerson College, where I studied teaching expository writing and won the Emerging Writer Award. My poetry, book reviews, and articles have been published in several magazines as well as on a popular reference website, www.helium.com. In my former job as a supervisor at a market research company, I'm often called upon to write, edit, or proofread reports; in previous administrative assistant positions at a nonprofit agency, a newspaper, and an accounting firm, I wrote business correspondence and task instructions. I've also edited and proofread freelance for the past ten years.

Each ensuing chapter of this book covers a particular aspect of writing for professionals: grammar, spelling, punctuation, word choice, sentence structure, paragraph structure, organization, the composition process, and the kinds of writing most often called for in a professional setting. I'll aim to discuss these subjects with a less academic, a lighter and more entertaining approach than the usual writing handbook. You'll get pointers on how to sell yourself on paper—and a good laugh.

Think of it as an investment in your future.

THE IMPORTANCE OF GRAMMAR IN WRITING BY PROFESSIONALS

In my first literature course as a freshman English major at the University of Maryland, we read an excerpt from Aristotle's *Poetics*. One of my classmates commented that she disapproved of Aristotle's axioms on writing poetry and drama because they "just limit creativity." Our instructor, a graduate student teaching assistant named Bill FitzGerald, responded with a question: "Is he being prescriptive or descriptive?" In other words, does Aristotle say, "You must do this when writing verse or plays," or does he say, "This characterizes most good verse and plays"? The answer is, of course, the latter.

The same holds true for the rules of grammar. Grammar serves not as a code of decrees by some self-appointed arbiter of taste, but as a description of how to create the most effective verbal communication possible—especially so in English, which has never had an official body like the *Académie Française* governing its development. No less an authority than *The Elements of Style* concurs: "The shape of our language is not rigid; in questions of usage we have no lawgiver whose word is final."

Since English has no central controlling force, where do our rules of grammar arise from? Bill Bryson provides the answer in his introduction to *Bryson's Dictionary of Troublesome Words*: "We are a messy democracy, and all the more delightful for it.... When we tire of a meaning or a usage or a spelling ... we change it, not by fiat but by consensus." We English-speakers follow the great Anglo-Saxon tradition of common law, of rules accepted by popular recognition. And what the people recognize in accepting them is simply that they work—that they make getting from one point in a sentence to another easier and clearer than any other option.

English grammar's origins in practicality and common agreement, its trial by the fire of everyday use, make it deserve our compliance more than the Ivory Tower formulations of other languages' official authorities, and make it more wayward to deviate from them in formal communication. Over time we may decide to repeal a grammatical decision made by earlier generations and replace it with one perhaps yet unthought of; Bill Bryson admits that change plays a part in our linguistic legislation. But it's often difficult to tell when a non-standard usage poises on the verge of overthrowing the old order and taking its rightful place as an ordinance of our language and when it is merely a widespread but transient aberration. As mentioned earlier, a variant usage will probably become standard only if it provides improvement in clarity or succinctness over its predecessor. To play it safe, until many works of reference on grammar or language note acceptance of a colloquial usage, leave it alone.

Grammar is especially important in business communication, where the clarity of your writing and the time it takes for your reader to understand it are vital. You should assume that your reader expects you to adhere to grammatical standards, because they are, after all, *standards*—the only ones we have for language. Grammar is the field within which the game of language is played. If the writer carries the ball out of bounds, the game stops because the reader can no longer follow the writer's thought; if the writer cannot consistently keep the ball inbounds, the reader may very well decide not to bother playing with someone who strays outside the collectively agreed-upon parameters without which communication would be impossible. We abide by the rules of grammar to keep the game running smoothly, without doubt and without delay.

I realize our language's hodgepodge of principles for distinguishing proper grammar can appear intimidating and labyrinthine, especially to those with more "real world" concerns preoccupying them most of the day. But exercising these principles really requires no skills that professionals don't exercise already. The same analytical and problem-solving skills, the same ability to categorize information and to read a situation that allows you to land a contract, win a case, or balance the books will enable you to use grammar correctly. Writing is very accommodating to transferring skills.

The parts of speech are the building blocks of grammar; their use and combination provides the subject of most grammar rules. A brief refresher on the parts of speech might prove useful as a preface to discussing grammar.

Noun: Person, place, thing, idea.
Verb: Action word.
Adjective: Describes a noun.
Adverb: Can describe verbs ("His mother *swiftly* kicked him in the rear."), adjectives ("The play was *painfully* boring."), or other adverbs ("The snow fell *somewhat* erratically.").
Conjunction: Connect phrases together: *and, or, but, yet,* and their ilk.
Prepositions: Relate things or actions to other things or actions in the sentence—by location, sequence, causation, or association. Words like *about, above, along, against, ahead, around, behind, because, below, beneath, down, for, from, of, off, over, to, toward,* and *with,* among many others, are prepositions.
Interjections: Single-word expressions of emotion, often exclamations: *Yes! No! Wow! Ugh. Yuck! Yikes! Oy vey!* (I know: that's not English. But you get the picture.)

Make sure to use parts of speech consistently; don't write a sentence like "This report breaks down the census findings ethnically, geographically, and with regards to income." This is the grammatical equivalent of wearing stripes and plaid. *Ethnically* and *geographically* are adverbs. Placing a prepositional phrase, "with regards to income," after them as the last term in the list ruins the expectation of consistency and parallel structure created by making the first two terms adverbs. Replace "with regards to income" with another adverb—*socioeconomically.*

You should particularly be careful with using parts of speech consistently in appositives, phrases that rename or define something mentioned earlier in the sentence. In *The New St. Martin's Handbook,* Andrea Lunsford and Robert Connors give this sentence as an example: "A stereotype is when someone characterizes a group unfairly." This sentence equates a noun (a thing—*stereotype*) with a verb (an action—*characterizes*). A thing, however, is not an event. The sentence would be improved by changing the verb in question to a noun: "A stereotype is an unfair characterization of a group."

Even when the appositive uses the same part of speech as its antecedent, make certain the term in the appositive corresponds to its antecedent in nature. Lunsford and Connors also offer this faulty sentence to consider: "A characteristic that I admire is a person who is generous." *Characteristic* and *person* are both nouns, but person is the wrong kind of noun—a characteristic is part of a person, not identical with him or her. The writer of this sentence emphasizes *generous,* an adjective; do what we did with the last sentence and make *generous* a noun, changing the sentence to "A characteristic that I admire is generosity."

8

Human beings instinctively crave pattern and order, so much so that this craving produced an entire field of study: Gestalt psychology, which gave us the Rorschach test. If your readers—be they clients, bosses, or colleagues—find that you create the expectation of pattern in your use of parts of speech but then undercut that pattern, they may find your writing hard to follow and your thinking hard to fathom.

Just as important as using parts of speech consistently is using them in the right place, especially modifiers. Because adverbs can be placed either before or after verbs they modify, they can create some confusion if placed near other parts of the sentence that they could conceivably modify. Lunsford and Connors counsel, "Be especially careful with the placement of limiting modifiers, like *almost, even, hardly, just, merely, nearly, only, scarcely,* and *simply*. In general, these modifiers should be placed right before the words they limit. Putting them anywhere else may produce not just ambiguity but a completely different meaning.

AMBIGUOUS	The court only hears civil cases on Tuesdays.
CLEAR	The court hears *only* civil cases on Tuesdays.
CLEAR	The court hears civil cases on Tuesdays *only*."

Lunsford and Connors picked the perfect modifier for their examples. *Only* probably poses the most difficulty in this regard because of its versatility: it's one of those adverbs that can modify verbs, adjectives, and other adverbs equally well, and additionally function as an adjective. Look at the example Bill Bryson provides in *Bryson's Dictionary of Troublesome Words*: "'The A Class bus only ran on Sundays' (*Observer*). Taken literally, the sentence suggests that on other days of the week the bus did something else—perhaps flew?" More realistically, it could also mean that no other bus but the A Class ran on Sundays, or that the A Class ran on Sunday and no other day. In the former case, "Only the A Class bus ran on Sundays" would nail down the meaning more effectively; in the latter, "The A Class bus ran on Sundays only." This last sentence illustrates (as does Lunsford and Connors' last example sentence) that *only* should, actually, be placed after what it modifies if it will be the final word in the sentence and if, by preceding what it modifies, *only* might be mistaken for modifying something else. Modifiers like *only* cue your reader in to points you want to emphasize; using them with precision ensures that your reader will pick up on the importance of what you see as important.

Another ambiguity trap lies in "understood" words—words that are implied but not actually written. Since poorly positioned words can create much confusion, unpositioned words can create even more, often when personal pronouns get involved. "When sentences with such constructions end in a pronoun," says *The New St. Martin's Handbook*, "the pronoun should be in the case it would be in if the construction were complete.
His brother has always been more athletic than *he* [is].
In some constructions like this, the case depends on the meaning intended. Use the subjective case if the pronoun is actually the subject of an omitted verb; use the objective case if it is an object of an omitted verb.

Willie likes Lily more than *she* [likes Lily].
Willie likes Lily more than [he likes] *her*."

"She" and "her," of course, are third parties.

Some sentences are better off including understood words; clarity needs to be bought at the expense of conciseness once in a while. Never assume your audience grasps your meaning in these cases (you know what happens when you assume). Put yourself in your audience's place. Would they possess the knowledge that would enable them to understand what you've left "understood?" If you're not certain, it doesn't hurt to spell out what you're referring to.

Come to think of it, knowing when to use subject and object pronouns creates a good deal of confusion when writing as well. As Kingsley Amis observes in *The King's English*, "The most common kind of mistake is to use the nominative [subject] form of a pronoun where common sense as well as grammar demand an oblique form, and write sentences like:
Everything good and pleasant in our lives we owe to He that loved us and died for us." *He* is the indirect object of the verb *owe* (He is not what we owe, He is to whom we owe it); the pronoun should really be *Him*. *He* is not the subject of the verbs *loved* and *died* because *that* intervenes between them, making everything afterwards a phrase modifying *He*—the sentence could survive grammatically without it. "Behind this example may be a feeling that *He* is posher than *Him*," Amis suggests, the reason presumably being that because subject pronouns normally come first in a sentence, they connote greater importance. But English grammar isn't modeled on dinner table seating order. It's based on common sense. Just look at the sentence. If what the pronoun refers to performs the sentence's action, make it a subject pronoun; if it receives the sentence's action, make it an object pronoun.
Bill Bryson calls a possible quandary to his reader's attention. Does one say "It was I who ..." or "It was me who ..."? There are arguments for both choices; the pronoun in question could be the subject of whatever verb follows *who*, or it could be the object of *was*. We can arrive at the solution by following one of the cardinal rules of writing, pithily and forcefully expressed by *The Elements of Style*: "Omit needless words." The construction "It was ... who" is pure verbal flab. Get rid of it, and we're left with the pronoun in question followed by the verb it performs. It then becomes clear that the sentence requires *I*, the subject pronoun.
This brings us to a special subtopic within subject and object pronouns that has haunted innumerable English-speakers: *who* versus *whom*. As usual, there are complications to the standard rule that *who* is the subject form and *whom* is the object form. *Bryson's Dictionary of Troublesome Words* points a major one out. Bryson notes that a sentence he happened upon somewhere, "'They rent it to whomever needs it,'" is incorrect; despite *whomever* serving as the indirect object of *rent*, it also serves as the subject of *needs*. Thus, *who* is used even for the subject of a subordinate phrase, not just for the subject of the whole sentence.

You know how almost everyone who pretends to care about such things tells you not to end a sentence with a preposition? Well, tell them to buzz off. That rule is grammar's version of an urban legend; Kingsley Amis calls it, with characteristic forthrightness, "one of those fancied prohibitions . . . dear to ignorant snobs." If I recall correctly, Bill Bryson's previous book *The Mother Tongue* (I have to rely on memory because the book appears to be out of print) tells us that this is actually a rule of Latin grammar that some pompous medieval scholastic tried to impose on English.
To arbitrarily avoid putting prepositions at the ends of sentences goes against the nature of our language. In English, achieving the clearest, most direct syntax possible sometimes necessitates making a preposition the last word. "Not only is the preposition acceptable at the end," affirm Strunk and White, "sometimes it is more effective in that spot than anywhere else."

For proof, think of the famous story about the editor who removed a preposition from the end of a sentence in one of Winston Churchill's speeches; Churchill dashed off an angry memorandum to him, warning, "This is the kind of arrant pedantry up with which I will not put!"

§

Most grammar problems in professional writing that I've come across revolve around verbs. Dealing with action, verbs are the most vital part of speech, and the heavy use that comes with indispensability makes them especially liable to pitfalls. Subject-verb agreement poses much of the trouble professionals have with grammar when writing.

The New St. Martin's Handbook locates the chief source of this trouble in other words intervening between the subject and the verb. In its example sentence, "A vase of flowers makes a room attractive," the third-person singular verb *makes* agrees with the subject, *vase. Of flowers* is only a prepositional phrase describing the subject, but to inexpert writers the position of the noun *flowers* next to the verb may become a red herring, throwing them off the scent of the real subject and causing them to use the plural verb *make*. Lunsford and Connors also counsel: "Be careful when you use phrases beginning with *as well as, along with, in addition to, together with,* or similar prepositions. They do not make a singular subject plural.

The president, along with many senators, *opposes* the bill."

The president is the sole subject of the sentence. *Along with many senators* serves as a parenthetical phrase, merely an incidental elaboration and not integral to the structure of the sentence. Thus, the sentence takes the singular verb *opposes* to agree with the singular subject "president."

To get this right, learn to recognize prepositional phrases—phrases beginning with words like *along, of, as, in, with,* and other words, which relate to and describe the subject. Most grammar textbooks and teachers advise that almost all prepositional phrases can be removed from the sentence while leaving it grammatically complete. We can demonstrate this truth on our example sentences from *The New St. Martin's Handbook*:

A vase makes a room attractive.
The president opposes the bill.

All a sentence needs grammatically to be complete is a subject and a verb that agrees with it in number. The vase still makes, and the president still opposes. Due to their removability, prepositional phrases don't count when considering grammatical number.

The picture complicates, however, when appositives enter it, especially when the appositive has more than one noun. As usual, *The New St. Martin's Handbook* sheds light on the problem:

"Carla is one of the employees who always work overtime.

Some employees always work overtime. Carla is among them. Thus *who* refers to *employees*, and the verb is plural." The sentence identifies Carla as doing the same thing as a group that she is part of; because her importance is subordinate to that of the group, the group is the actual subject of *work*. On the other hand,

"Sam is the only one of the employees who always works overtime."

Only one employee always works overtime, and that employee is Sam. Thus *one*, and not *employees,* is the antecedent of *who*, and the verb form is singular." Sam does something different from the rest of the group he is part of; he is described in contradistinction to the group, and therefore Sam is the subject of *works*.

Other challenges arise with other kinds of subjects, including compound subjects, which include more than one noun. Lunsford and Connors write, "When subjects joined by *and* are considered a single unit or refer to the same person or thing, they take a singular verb form.

John Kennedy's closest friend and political ally was his brother."
For an easy way to figure this one out, flip the subject and the direct object: "His brother was John Kennedy's closest friend and political ally." The singular verb *was* clearly still works with the simple singular subject *brother*; this formation illustrates that *friend* and *ally* refer to the same person. The most prevalent instances of compound subjects considered a single unit are companies or performance groups: Standard and Poor, Procter and Gamble, Sanford and Son, Peaches and Herb, Cheech and Chong.

Lunsford and Connors continue: "If the word *each* or *every* precedes subjects joined by *and*, the verb form is singular.

Each boy and girl *chooses* one gift to take home."

Each and *every* particularize all members of a group. You could say these words make all individual members of a group the subject of the sentence simultaneously. Bill Bryson observes that compound subjects joined by *or* are more straightforward: "Whereas *and* draws diverse elements together, *or* keeps them separate. When all the elements are singular, the verb should be singular too. . . . When there are a mixture of singulars and plurals, the rule is to make the verb agree with the noun or pronoun nearest it."

Also straightforward are collective nouns, nouns consisting of several individual things but considered as a single aggregate whole. Since they emphasize the sum of the parts, collective nouns just about always take singular verbs: "A flock of geese flies hundreds of miles when the seasons change." As simple as this is, some grammarians insist on complicating it. Lunsford and Connors write, "Collective nouns can take either singular or plural verb forms, depending on whether they refer to the group as a single unit or the multiple members of the group." Lunsford and Connors again provide an example sentence to back up their claim: "The jury still disagree on a number of counts." This is just stupid. I have never heard anyone— ANYONE—say "The jury still disagree." If you want to refer to the multiple members of the group, use a plural noun, not the collective noun: "The jurors still disagree on a number of counts."

They do get it right about indefinite subjects, which are usually pronouns and "do not refer to specific persons or things"—at least, those persons or things are not named in the sentence. "Most take singular verb forms.... *Both, few, many, others,* and *several* are plural." For obvious reasons. In addition, "*All, any, enough, more, most, none,* and *some* can be singular or plural, depending on the noun they refer to." For instance, referring to spices, "Any seasons

12

meat wonderfully" emphasizes that every individual spice in the collection alluded to works well, while "Any season meat wonderfully" connotes that all the several spices that make up the range referred to work well.

Another frequent writing error involving verbs is shifting tenses over the course of a composition. A friend of mine related to me that for a project in his English class as a sophomore in high school, he and his classmates had to grade one another's short stories; even in what should have been quite straightforward narratives, his classmates could not keep their tenses consistent. "I would literally get dizzy reading them" from confusion over when the events of the stories were happening in relation to one another, he said. Then again, he does happen to have diabetes, so maybe it was just insulin shock. That possibility notwithstanding, while professional writing often seeks to elicit a specific reaction from the reader, vertigo generally does not rank high among them.

The New St. Martin's Handbook reminds us, "General truths or scientific facts should be in the simple present, even when the predicate of the sentence is in the past tense.

Pasteur demonstrated that his boiling process makes milk safe."

Note that this sentence has two verbs: Pasteur demonstrated his process in the past, but the process still makes milk safe today, so *makes* is in the present tense. Also, when discussing literature of any sort, use the present tense. Although the literature was written in the past, it continues to speak to us in the present. By way of example, I wrote in a recent e-mail, "As Othello says, 'Alas, I have loved fondly [i.e., foolishly] and too well.'" If I wanted to emphasize the author rather than the character, I would have written, "As Shakespeare writes ..." (Never you mind what I was writing about.)

The Elements of Style makes the simple declaration: "In summaries, keep to one tense." But summaries sometimes prove not so simple. At my job, I once wrote and edited summaries of focus group discussions for a certain company on a proposed new product with a project manager; she knew she had a problem with shifting tenses and instructed me to keep an eye out for them. The complication lay in that the summaries did not include only things said and done during the focus group itself—participants spoke about their personal histories and current practices with similar products. I gave her some simple rules of thumb. Whatever happened at the focus group and/or previously should take the past tense, and whatever is ongoing and still happens now that the focus group is over should take the present tense. Very few actions were mentioned that would definitely begin after the focus group, but these would have taken the future tense. Actions that were possible after the focus group, like the participants trying the proposed product, took the conditional form, using constructions like *would try, may be willing,* or *might consider.*

Dangling participles pose another major threat to writing by professionals. Participles are verb forms, usually ending in *-ing,* that express an action concurrent with the main verb of the sentence; grammatically, though, they function as adjectives describing a noun in the sentence. Participles dangle when they grammatically refer to the wrong noun, as in Strunk and White's example: "Being in a dilapidated condition, I was able to buy the house very cheap." As the sentence stands, the speaker states that he or she is dilapidated, when he or she wants to describe the house, the direct object, as dilapidated.

Dangling participles occur most often when, as in the sentence above, they are placed out of their normal order at the beginning of a sentence—in which case, Strunk and White indicate, they must refer to the subject of the sentence. Their example sentence can easily be recast correctly: "I was able to buy the house, being in a dilapidated condition, very cheap." Moving the participial phrase to the middle of the sentence frees it to modify the noun it follows.

In *The King's English*, the late British novelist Kingsley Amis offers the following excerpt to illustrate that writers often lapse into dangling participles when what they are supposed to modify is not the main focus of the writer's or reader's attention:

"Sheridan was once staying at the home of an elderly maiden lady who wanted more of his attention than he was willing to give. Proposing one day to take a stroll with him, he excused himself on account of the badness of the weather."... It was clearly the elderly maiden lady who proposed the stroll but, far from being the subject of the second sentence, she appears in the preceding one and there only in a subordinate capacity. Today, and yesterday too, even a not-over-careful writer would have felt constrained to begin the second sentence with a phrase like "When she proposed" or "On her proposing."

Having seen these examples, I think we can readily agree with Amis: "The objection to the unattached or wrongly attached participle is firstly, of course, that it is unprofessional, the sign of a casual or careless writer. Secondly, though not often truly ambiguous, it may cause the attentive reader (the only sort really worth having) to pause without profit, to spend some unnecessary time checking that the sentence in question and its constituent parts are as they seemed to be." The attentive readers of professionals have, sadly, less attention and time to spend than most, and thus professionals have less leeway for their misuse of participles.

Participles can also modify nouns without an accompanying phrase behind them, as in the sentences "The train came to a grinding halt" and "The grinding train came to a halt." Keep in mind, however, that not all -*ing* verbs function as adjectives. They can fill another office: nouns. Gerunds are -*ing* verbs turned into nouns, as in the sentence "The grinding of the train as it stopped annoyed us"; here, *grinding* refers to an action as a thing, a phenomenon. Last but not least, they can work as actual verbs, as in "The train was grinding to a halt."

The subjunctive mood is the last major area in which verbs cause problems for professionals in their writing, probably because most of us forget what it is. English verbs have three grammatical moods. The most common is the indicative mood, which deals with simple statements of events; the imperative, the other mood that most people know, uses the verb in a command. The subjunctive mood expresses possible, desired, or conditional actions. *The New St. Martin's Handbook* provides a handy-dandy list of sentences illustrating each of the moods:

"INDICATIVE   I *did* the right thing.
IMPERATIVE   *Do* the right thing.
SUBJUNCTIVE   If I *had done* the right thing, I would not be in trouble
                  now."

The subjunctive is much less memorable in English than in other languages because it does not have its own unique conjugation in our language. "The present subjunctive uses the base form," write Lunsford and Connors—the infinitive form without *to* in front of it. If we

14

turned their sample subjunctive sentence from past tense into present, it would be "If I do the right thing, I will not be in trouble." The other verb in the sentence takes the future tense because, of course, it is the consequence of the subjunctive verb. Actually, the present tense works as the future subjunctive as well; only context would determine whether "If I do the right thing" refers to acting immediately or after the passage of some time. "The past subjunctive is the same as the past tense," Lunsford and Connors continue, "except for the verb *be*, which uses *were* for all subjects." For some reason, they use the past perfect in their sample sentence, but the subjunctive mood works equally well in the simple past: "If I did the right thing, I would not be in trouble right now."

Most of the trick to getting the subjunctive right lies in recognizing when it must be used. *The New St. Martin's Handbook* digests these situations:

- clauses expressing a wish
- *If* clauses expressing a condition that does not exist
- *as if* and *as though* clauses
- *that* clauses expressing a demand, request, requirement, or suggestion

Hence, Bill Bryson correctly argues that the verb in this sentence from Britain's *Daily Mail* should really be *consider*: "'The Senate has now rewritten the contract insisting that the Navy considers other options' . . ." The clause beginning with "that," which the verb in question is part of, expresses the Senate's demand upon the Navy; the verb must take the subjunctive mood. *The New St. Martin's Handbook* also diagnoses another reason why people mess up on the subjunctive: "Because the subjunctive can create a rather formal tone, many people today tend to substitute the indicative in informal conversation.

If I *was* a better typist, I would type my own papers."

As mentioned above, the past subjunctive of "to be" is always "were." "Nevertheless," the *Handbook* insists, "formal writing still requires the use of the subjunctive ..." Your co-workers and clients would probably recognize that "If I were a better typist" would correctly begin Lunsford and Connors's example sentence above; maybe not all of them would recognize that the word *if* at the beginning of the phrase makes the difference between *was* and *were*, and fewer still might name the form involved as the subjunctive mood. Yet reading "If I was" wouldn't sit well with them. The writing would feel less than smooth, and awkwardness does not make someone confident in doing business with you.

To give you some relief from all this conceptual complexity, I'll discuss a much simpler area now: the split infinitive. Guess what? There's no rule against it. In *The King's English*, Kingsley Amis calls it "the best known of the imaginary rules that petty linguistic tyrants seek to lay upon the English language." They are indeed petty, for Bill Bryson notes "the curiously persistent belief that the split infinitive is widely condemned by authorities. That ... is untrue. Almost no authority flatly condemns it." Even the sacrosanct *Elements of Style* informs us, "There is precedent from the fourteenth century down for interposing an adverb between *to* and the infinitive it governs," but it then immediately cautions that "the construction should be avoided unless the writer wishes to place unusual stress on the adverb.

to diligently inquire   to inquire diligently"

In Strunk and White's former sample phrase, the position of the adverb before the verb emphasizes the manner of the inquiry; in the latter, where the adverb trails after the verb, the emphasis rests on the act of inquiring itself. The first phrase might be used in a press release for damage control after an explosion at a manufacturing plant for toxic chemicals to assure the public that the company is taking responsibility, the second in an ordinary internal activity report on an important project to convey a sense of proper follow-through. Don't be shy about splitting an infinitive with an adverb when its emphasis is duly desired. Would *Star Trek* have become such a massive pop culture phenomenon if the Starship *Enterprise*'s mission statement had ended: " ... to go boldly where no man has gone before"?

A true error related to the infinitive grows disgustingly common: writing *try and* followed by another verb, rather than *try to*. *The Elements of Style* categorically rules: "*Try*. Takes the infinitive: 'try to mend it,' not 'try and mend it.'" *Bryson's Dictionary of Troublesome Words* concedes that the phrase *try and* is "no longer resisted as strenuously as it once was," but holds that it "is still widely regarded as colloquial by many authorities and is thus better avoided in serious writing." It's not just colloquial, it flies in the face of fundamental English grammar—so much so that my father, who didn't go to college, complained to me on the telephone when he read an article containing the phrase in the Washington *Post*. *Try* is one of those classic auxiliary verbs, like *want* or *hope*, that combine with the infinitive of another verb to express effort toward or anticipation of an action.

We might all use *try and* in conversation sometimes. But until people start saying, "I am going and run in the marathon tomorrow," it will remain just plain wrong. Using it in professional writing will make your reader think you're a moron, and making your superiors, clients, peers, or even subordinates think you're a moron has never been a fast track to career advancement.

§

My personal grammatical pet peeve—one of the few that doesn't directly pertain to parts of speech—is the misuse of the possessive suffix. As far as I can tell, this rampant habit arose only during the last 12 to 15 years, and I can trace its cause to nothing but an exponential increase in linguistic stupidity and carelessness among those with a good deal of formal learning. Let me summarize the simple rules governing the possessive suffix, drawn in large part from *The Elements of Style*:

- For most singular nouns—including those ending in *s*—and for plural nouns that don't end in *s*, add apostrophe-*s*.
  Pandora's box, Charles's dog, the children's room
- For ancient names ending in *s*, add an apostrophe.
  Moses' time, Aeschylus' plays, Achilles' heel
- For plural nouns ending in *s*, add an apostrophe.
  his friends' advice, the Robinsons' house
- For more than one noun, add apostrophe-*s* to only the last noun if they are considered a single unit, but add apostrophe-*s* to all of them if they are considered individually.
  Standard and Poor's ratings, Ripken's and Murray's careers

Strunk and White add, "A common error is to write *it's* for *its*, or vice versa. The first is a contraction, meaning 'it is.' The second is a possessive [adjective].

It's a wise dog that scratches its own fleas."

Because we're used to dealing with apostrophe-*s* in possessives, we often automatically associate it with the possessive when using *its*. All it takes to overcome this mistake is a moment of critical thinking.

There is, on the other hand, absolutely no excuse for any college-educated person to use an apostrophe in a plural, *à la* "word's," which I have seen numerous times in professionals' writing. I find this "greengrocer's apostrophe"—so called, according to Lynne Truss in her invaluable best-selling treatise *Eats, Shoots and Leaves*, because it was once liberally used on market-stall signs by unlettered produce vendors in England—the most perplexing manifestation of the incorrect possessive. Those guilty must live in total oblivion to their surroundings; you'll never see a plural apostrophized in print media, on billboards, on television, or in the supermarket—not even in the produce section. In this regard, at least, grocers have exceeded their more lucratively-employed customers in literacy.

The opposite offense also arises frequently: omitting possessive apostrophes where they belong. Truss cites the title of the film *Two Weeks Notice* ("... if it were 'one week's notice' there would be an apostrophe"). I was a member of an organization in my hometown called the Greenbelt Writers Group. It bore this name because a majority of the membership couldn't decide how *Writers* should be made possessive—even though the group by definition contained more than one writer, meaning an apostrophe should have gone after the *s*. As a result, we looked to the world like we had no idea how to do the activity that brought us together.

The rules of the possessive suffix are not rocket science; most of what the typical white-collar worker does on the job is a lot more conceptually complex. If you can't keep your apostrophes straight, your clients and bosses will likely wonder whether you can keep your performance and priorities straight. Forget about the excuse that conventions like this are mere window-dressing and that all your readers know what you mean anyway. If that were true, Lynne Truss wonders, "Why ... would they open a large play area for children, hang up a sign saying 'Giant Kid's Playground,' and wonder why everyone stays away from it? (Answer: everyone is scared of the Giant Kid.)" Like all conventions of language, the possessive suffix was instituted to facilitate communication. It would not exist if unneeded.

When all these grammatical rules are laid out and explained, they probably seem more complex than they really are. Most of us instinctively get them right most of the time, because they are part of the background fabric of our wonderfully supple language that we internalize one way or another—we have an ear for them. But when we don't know the principles behind this feeling for grammar, we may second-guess our ears. And professionals in particular may not have time to leaf through reference books to assuage their doubts. Don't worry: that's why I'm here.

PREVENTING COMMON SPELLING MISTAKES

I shouldn't have to write this chapter.

And no, not because of spell-check. Too many of us forget the imperfections of word-processing software features for checking spelling. They usually cannot find misused homonyms, like *to* or *two* where *too* belongs, as Angela Lunsford and Robert Connors note in *The New St. Martin's Handbook*; in a recent study of spelling skills, Lunsford and Connors write, "Students using spell checkers misspelled almost as many words as did students who handwrote or typed their essays." Spell-checkers furnish a great way to perform easy corrections before looking for more subtle mistakes yourself. But all professionals should possess as fundamental a language skill as spelling, and spell-checkers should not become a crutch to support poor knowledge of it—because they're not foolproof, eventually the truth will out.

We'll start our discussion of spelling with careless mistakes, ones that nobody in a professional position should make. Yet, in my experience, a significant number do.

Due. I have seen this word spelled *do* more than once in professional writing I have edited, and it almost made me gag. A sure bellwether of laziness and inattention while writing. Anyone caught making this mistake in finished writing should be fired on the spot.

Morale. As Kingsley Amis indicates in *The King's English*, *morale* is a noun meaning something like high spirits or willingness, and confidence in one's ability, to perform necessary duties. "Moral" is an adjective meaning "ethical." When one writes about "the need to raise employee moral," one seems not only to use the wrong part of speech but also to defame the character of one's entire staff.

Their, There, and They're. A completely inexcusable, but frighteningly frequent, mistake. *Their* is a possessive adjective; it means "belonging to them." *There* is a demonstrative pronoun, the opposite of *here*. *They're* is a contraction of *they are*. It's a pronoun and verb combined. These words differ greatly in meaning and grammatical function—the only thing they have in common is how they sound. When writing, you shouldn't focus only on your words as you hear them in your head: pay attention to the paper or screen you write on and to how the words LOOK that you write on it.

Let's go on to more complex spelling errors whose commission is more forgivable.

Accommodate. Bill Bryson, author of *Bryson's Dictionary of Troublesome Words*, bids us to note that the word has two *m*'s. Just think of the *commode*, where we enjoy the most primal comfort of all.

Definite. Often misspelled *definate*, and its adverbial form *definately*. Lunsford and Connors suggest thinking of the word's relation to *finite*. If something is definite, the possibility of its existence has been determined and thereby limited.

Deserts. I don't mean the Sahara and the Mojave. I mean the word as used in the phrase "just deserts," with the stress on the second syllable. In *The King's English*, Kingsley Amis warns us not to spell it like *desserts*; although the words are pronounced the same way, "just deserts" comes from *deserve*. Spell it accordingly.

Homogeneous. Amis points out the *e* in the suffix—it's not "homogenous."

Idiosyncrasy. Bryson calls attention to the next-to-last letter being an *s* rather than a *c*. I think the problem stems from how, in speaking, we commonly aspirate that second *s* the way we do all soft *c*'s but not all *s*'s.

Minuscule. The second vowel is often mistakenly written as an *i*. Bryson advises, "Think of *minus*, not *mini*."

Plenitude. "Not *plenti-*," writes Bill Bryson about this word meaning fullness or abundance. To remember this, know that the word does not come from *plenty*, but instead from *plein*, the French word for "full."

Supersede. "Even quite good people, for instance, sometimes write *supercede* instead of the correct *supersede*," Kingsley Amis observes. The suffixes *-cede* or *-ceed* mean to go. *Precede* means to go before and *succeed* to go after. Thus, we tend to think of movement as progressing forward from lesser to greater importance; *supercede* would mean to go above, which violates the horizontal forward movement model. The suffix *-sede*, however, comes from the Latin *sedere*, "to sit"—it pertains to position, which we tend to think of as progressing upwards from lesser to greater importance. *Supersede*, then, means to sit above, i.e., to occupy a position of greater importance.

The New St. Martin's Handbook reviews some spelling rules. Undoubtedly, the most famous spelling rule in English is "*i* before *e* except after *c*"—even as I write, I can hear Snoopy playing the mouth harp in the song about this rule on the Charlie Brown cartoon. Most words containing *ei* after *c* are verbs whose noun forms contain the *e* but not the *i*; *receive* becomes *reception*, *deceive* becomes *deception*. In a major exception to the rule that Lunsford and Connors note, *e* precedes *i* when the diphthong is pronounced as *ay*, as in *eight, neighbor, reign, weigh*. The rule also does not apply to certain "weird" exceptions, as Lunsford and Connors call them: "ancient, caffeine, conscience, either, foreign, height, leisure, neither, science, seize, species," and, weirdly enough, "weird" itself. Examining these words closely, though, we can discover a method to the madness of some of them. In *science*, the *i* and the *e* belong to different syllables. *Conscience*, derived from *science*, was originally pronounced like it; now, its *i*, and that in *ancient* and *species*, isn't really pronounced at all, but rather changes the preceding *c* from its normal pronunciation. In *caffeine*, the first *e* is part of the root word derived from *coffee* and the *i* begins the suffix. Lastly, the *ei* in *either* can't follow a *c* because it's at the beginning of the word, and *neither* is simply its negative formed by adding *n* in front of it—like *nor* from *or* and *naught* from *aught*.

Most of the other spelling rules that *The New St. Martin's Handbook* covers have to do with suffixes. First, "For words ending in an unpronounced *e*…. In general, if a suffix starts with a vowel, drop the *e*," it prescribes. "If the suffix starts with a consonant, keep the *e*." For instance, *debatable* and *hateful*. As usual in English, where there's a rule, there are exceptions:

"dye + -ing = dyeing	marriage + -able = marriageable
notice + -able = noticeable	courage + -ous = courageous
argue + -ment = argument	true + -ly = truly
judge + -ment = judgment	nine + -th = ninth . . ."

We retain the *e* in *dyeing* to distinguish it from *dying*—a drastically different action. In *noticeable*, we leave the *e* in to keep the *c* soft; the same principle operates for the *g* in *marriageable* and *courageous*. The *e* in *ninth* is dropped to keep it silent, as in the root word, because it would normally be pronounced between two consonants.

The next rule pertains to a topic that, I confess, perplexed me until not too long ago: doubling the last letter of a word when adding a suffix. "When a suffix beginning with a vowel is added to a word that ends in a consonant," Lunsford and Connors write, "the consonant is sometimes doubled. In general, if the word ends in consonant + vowel + consonant and the word contains only one syllable or ends in an accented syllable, double the final consonant.

stop + -ing = stopping   begin + -ing = beginning . . ."

Therefore, we spell *traveled* and *counseled* with one *l* because the root word's first, not its last, syllable is stressed. Moreover, we don't double the *d* in *ending* or *reprimanding* because the root word ends in two consecutive consonants, as opposed to two consonants separated by a vowel.

As a child, I was taught that words ending with *o* take the plural suffix *-es*. Like many things taught to us in our early lives, this rule proved only partially true, as *The New St. Martin's Handbook* demonstrates: "Add *–es* if the *o* is preceded by a consonant. Add *–s* if the *o* is preceded by a vowel.

potato, potatoes
radio, radios . . ."

Words of foreign origin form an exception to this expanded rule, as in the title of Ezra Pound's Italian-flavored *Pisan Cantos*.

English is one of the world's most irregular languages, and its orthography is a chief factor in its irregularity. We extracted some patterns and guidelines from the exceptions to its spelling rules, but they only covered a few of those exceptions. English spelling, for the most part, challenges the writer to master it through carefully studying and immersing himself or herself in the written language.

How does a writer do that? *The New St. Martin's Handbook* offers a few techniques. Try associating the word in question with other words, possibly words related to it. I did that for many of the words listed earlier; as noted above, the example of *definite* came from the *Handbook*. Lunsford and Connors explain why this technique might be particularly helpful in certain cases:

In English words, *a, i,* and *e* often sound alike in syllables that are not stressed. Hearing the word *definite*, for instance, gives us few clues as to whether the vowels in the second and third syllables should be *i*'s or *a*'s. In this case, remembering how the related word *finite* looks or sounds helps us to know that the *i*'s are correct.

This technique, concentrating on sound, would probably work best for auditory learners.

They also recommend, "Learning to 'see' words with unpronounced letters and syllables will help you spell them correctly." This was my strategy in my early teens as a spelling bee champion. I would look at the words I had trouble with printed on my study sheet until I could see the word spelled correctly with my mind's eye. If you come across a word while reading that you have found difficult to spell, follow the sequence of letters with your eyes until you brand it into your memory. Obviously, this method would work best for visual learners.

If these mental devices don't work, Lunsford and Connors point us to the best device of all: "Then check your dictionary."

Both Amis and *The New St. Martin's Handbook* touch on words written as compound words in certain circumstances and as two separate words in others. These occasionally compounded word pairs usually function as modifiers when written as single words, but can be any part of speech when written separately. *The New St. Martin's Handbook* gives examples:

"Of course, they did not wear *everyday* clothes *every day* of the year. . . .
We *may be* on time for the meeting, or *maybe* we won't!"

Everyday is an adjective describing *clothes*, and *maybe* is an adverb modifying *won't* [*will not*]. On the other hand, *every day* is an adjective and a noun, and *may be* is a compound verb. Be sure not to use these compound words outside of their role as modifiers, for, as Amis writes, "*come to lunch sometime* is deplorable . . . but *a sometime* [i.e., former] *academic* is acceptable ..."

Incidentally, I should reiterate Lunsford and Connors's axiom that *cannot* should always be written as one word. I can't explain why the words *can* and *not* were rolled into one, but they were. Deal with it.

Before closing, I'd like to comment on spelling in e-mail. The immediacy of this medium can lead writers to approach it more casually than they would snail-mail and to take liberties with spelling—although I suspect intentional misspelling and unnecessary abbreviations crept into e-mail from instant messaging, in which participants often try to simulate the pace of spoken conversation. But, as its name implies, e-mail was modeled after good old-fashioned written correspondence, and one should be as careful about correct spelling in business communication conducted by e-mail as one would with any professional document transmitted on paper.

What I have written in previous chapters about other aspects of professional writing equally applies to spelling: it impacts both the intelligibility of your message and its standing with your audience. The rules of spelling and of other aspects of writing are linguistic codicils of the social contract. Society must have certain ground rules for verbal communication in order for the writer to translate his or her individual perspective into the common understanding of humanity; Bill Bryson declares that "we all agree that clarity is better served if *cup* represents a drinking vessel and *cap* something you put on your head ..." Incorrect spelling, in its small but insidious way, can lead the audience to conclude that the writer does not know the ground rules well enough to accomplish this translation, and this ignorance can in turn imply that the writing's substance lacks the sophistication to warrant serious consideration.

THE FUNCTION AND USE OF PUNCTUATION

I won't bemoan the poor state of punctuation in contemporary professional writing, as I have done with the topics of my previous articles. British writer Lynne Truss provides plenty of nauseating examples of punctuation's misuse in her book *Eats, Shoots and Leaves,* a delightfully discursive exploration of the rationale of punctuation. Offering a guide to punctuation entails covering a lot of ground; I'll stick to providing an overview and explanation of proper use of punctuation.

After all, good reasons exist for confusion about punctuation—although not all punctuation mistakes can be attributed to a good reason. First, we have a lot of it. Biblical Hebrew, by contrast, only uses one punctuation mark, a pair of dots similar to our colon at the end of a verse. This lack of internal punctuation plays a part in the Bible's delicious ambiguity and in the richness and variety of commentary on it. But it became evident that for more mundane matters a larger repertoire of punctuation was needed, and Modern Hebrew adopted the same system of punctuation used in other Western languages. With the advantage of having more marks to choose from comes the burden of remembering when and why to choose each one.

Another major reason for confusion in using punctuation is its dual purpose. Lynne Truss writes in *Eats, Shoots and Leaves* of "the mixed origins of modern punctuation, and its consequent mingling of two quite distinct functions:

1   To illuminate the grammar of a sentence
2   To point up ... such literary qualities as rhythm, diction, pitch, tone and flow."

On the one hand, punctuation marks hold together the syntax and conceptual structure of a sentence. "Some grammarians use the analogy of stitching: 'punctuation as the basting that holds the fabric of language in shape,'" Truss writes. She also cites the writer Eric Partridge's description of punctuation as "'the line along which the train (composition, style, writing) must travel if it isn't to run away with its driver.'" By regulating a sentence's structure and relationship among ideas, punctuation also regulates its meaning. As proof, Truss presents us with two sentences that, differing only in their punctuation, have exactly opposite meanings:

"A woman, without her man, is nothing.
A woman: without her, man is nothing."

On the other hand, punctuation marks also reflect how we speak, how we would say a sentence aloud; they represent the pauses and variations in tone and inflection of voice we make in speech. In fact, Truss observes, "For a millennium and a half, punctuation's purpose was to guide actors, chanters, and readers-aloud through stretches of manuscript, indicating the pauses, accentuating matters of sense and sound, and leaving syntax mostly to look after itself." She makes the same analogy that Gail Mazur, my poetry workshop instructor in graduate school at Emerson College, made in discussing punctuation: "Punctuation directs you how to read, in the way musical notation directs a musician how to play." It serves a physical as well as a mental function.

According to Truss, only the development of printing and the consequent mass growth of literacy gave rise to punctuation's syntactical function. With more and more people writing, language needed a standard way to govern how it was written. This standardization wasn't complete until the late 19th Century. Before then, one could commonly see two punctuation marks combined in the same place, such as a colon or semicolon with a dash; punctuation marks such as dashes strewn repeatedly through a single sentence; or other usages that today would seem outlandish. Some may say standardization of punctuation has hampered individual expression, but I believe it's more likely it has fostered clearer comprehension of what writers express.

The most fundamental punctuation mark—and the simplest to discuss—is the period. It signals the end of a sentence, the completion of a whole thought. In speaking, it is exactly what the British term for it suggests: a "full stop." The speaker pauses long enough to inhale and exhale. *Eats, Shoots and Leaves* notes that traditionally typists leave two spaces after a period, probably to emphasize its finality and its subsequent long breath, but that a single space afterwards has become increasingly accepted.

Question marks carry an equally obvious function. One should remember, however, that question marks should not be used for indirect questions, ones that state a condition of doubt or uncertainty without taking the interrogative form—or, as Angela Lunsford and Robert Connors in *The New St. Martin's Handbook* put it, "which report rather than ask questions.

I asked how the child was.
Many parents ask if autism is an inherited disorder."

I have a problem with Lynne Truss's example of an indirect question, however: "What was the point of all this sudden interest in Brussels, he wondered." This question is not so much indirect as internal, being part of someone's thoughts rather than of his or her actual discourse. Grammatically, it takes the form of a question, complete with the question word "what." One could just as correctly replace the comma after *Brussels* with a question mark and italicize all the preceding words to label them as thought rather than spoken speech.

We tend to raise our voices noticeably on the first syllable of a question, and then slightly on the last syllable. The best example of this pattern that comes to my mind is a line from the movie *Lawrence of Arabia*. Lawrence mentions General Allenby's advance on Jerusalem to the general; Allenby retorts, "AM I going to Jerusa-lem?"

The exclamation point conveys emphasis, connoting that the sentence bursts out of us under the pressure of our enthusiasm. Its function is much more vocal than structural—we tend to raise our voices for the last stressed syllable of an exclamation—and therefore is better used in reporting direct speech than in deliberately written discourse. For professional writing especially, one should use the exclamation point as little as possible. If your ideas and words don't have the strength and power to hit the reader between the eyes, a little vertical line added above the period won't do the job for them. Indeed, sometimes one makes the boldest impression with a blunt, plain statement, for example: "During December 1942, one German soldier was killed in Stalingrad every seven seconds." If the previous sentence ended in an exclamation point instead of a period, the sentence would carry an almost juvenile excess excitement.

Things get much more complicated with the comma. Of all punctuation marks, it leaves the most room for subjectivity in its application. Truss explains, "When it comes to improving the clarity of a sentence, you can nearly always argue that one should go in; you can nearly always argue that one should come out. Stylists have meanwhile always dickered with the rules: Oscar Wilde famously spent all day over a completed poem, dangling a questionable comma over it ..."

Eats, Shoots and Leaves contains the best set of guidelines for using commas I've ever seen. First, it tackles using commas to separate items in a list. "The rule here is that the comma is correct if it can be replaced by *and* or *or*," it declares. A question arises, then, about whether to use a comma after the next-to-last item in a list, since *and* or *or* follows it. Truss says that American usage includes the comma while British usage leaves it out. To the British, rebelling against their heritage of starchy formalism, a comma in this position feels posh; Truss calls it "the Oxford comma." I myself am a stickler for it, but my company's house style for writing reports omits the comma before *and*. Truss does say, "British grammarians will concede that sometimes the extra comma prevents confusion" for exactly the same reason I insist on using it, "as when there are other *and*s in the vicinity:

> I went to the chemist, Marks & Spencer, and NatWest.
> I went to NatWest, the chemist, and Marks & Spencer."

Without the last commas in the two sentences above, the preponderance of the word *and* would make it difficult to determine where one unit of the list ends and another begins.
Moreover, Truss cautions against separating certain combinations of adjectives with commas: "But you should NOT use a comma for:

> It was an endangered white rhino.
> Australian red wines are better than Australian white ones....

This is because, in each of these cases, the adjectives do their jobs in joyful combination; they are not intended as a list." More accurately, the second of these adjectives combines with the noun to designate a certain category of that noun. The white rhino is a known species of rhinoceros; red and white wines are known types of wines. The first adjectives in the combinations specify qualities of the nouns not inherent in their particular categories. By contrast, one would include a comma in the sentence "The sheep gave a dull, pitiful bleat." There are no classes of sheep noises labeled *pitiful* or *dull*. These adjectives simply identify independent qualities of the particular sound made by the sheep in that instance.

One context does exist for always using a comma just before *and*. "Commas are used when two complete sentences are joined together, using such conjunctions as *and, or, but, while* and *yet*," writes Truss. She continues, "But trouble arises with this joining-comma rule from two directions: when stylists deliberately omit the conjunction and just keep the comma where a semicolon is called for (this is the 'splice comma' ...), and when the wrong joining words are used." I'll discuss where semicolons belong and which transition words should follow them in the next section. For now, suffice it to restrict yourselves to the conjunctions named by Truss when following a comma to join two grammatically complete sentences into one. The use of a comma to do so without such a conjunction is called a "comma splice" because the comma alone, as a mere pause, isn't strong enough to accomplish the task; without the proper mechanics to hold the sentence's two independent clauses together, its meaning bifurcates and falls apart. Next, commas play the role of *"filling gaps.... involving missing words cunningly implied by a comma:*

> Annie had dark hair; Sally, fair."

For conciseness, the comma replaces *had* in its coordinate position in the second clause of the sentence, serving as a compromise between parallel structure and repetitiveness.

Commas also precede quotes introduced by the formula "So-and-so said" or an equivalent:

> The policeman yelled, "Get back here!"

Do not place a comma before a quotation "when a quotation is introduced by *that* or when the rest of the sentence includes more than the words used to introduce or identify the source of the quotation," says *The New St. Martin's Handbook*. It gives these sentences as illustration:

> "The writer of Ecclesiastes concludes that 'all is vanity.'
> People who say 'Have a nice day' irritate me."

Although the quotation in the second sentence is directly preceded by the verb *say*, the quotation itself does not refer to an instance of direct speech but to a commonly repeated phrase. *Rules of Thumb for Business Writers*, by Diana Roberts Wienbroer et al., concurs with *The New St. Martin's Handbook* about quotations following the word *that*, and frames other occasions where a comma would not introduce a quote in terms of weaving the quote into the fabric of your own text. "For short quotations," it advises, "... don't put a comma before the quotation. Simply use the writer's phrase as it fits smoothly into your sentence:

> Robert finds it essential to 'restrain the individual somewhat' for the sake of orderly discussion."

In sum, introduce a quote with a comma only when it does not fit structurally into the flow of your own writing—when someone hearing your writing aloud could tell, because of a meaningful pause beforehand, that another "voice" is speaking.

Truss's next rule for commas is for setting off interjections within sentences:

> "Blimey, what would we do without it?
> Stop, or I'll scream."

Truss's sentences begin with interjections. Nonetheless, a comma can set off an interjection at the end of a sentence: "It's cold in here, man!"

Pairs of commas enclose certain kinds of semi-parenthetical phrases. These are asides, phrases you might lower your voice for or speak more quickly, returning to your natural speaking voice afterwards. Lynne Truss describes their function in writing: "The commas mark the places where the reader can—as it were—place an elegant two-pronged fork and cleanly lift out a section of the sentence, leaving no obvious damage to the whole." They usually enclose nonrestrictive clauses. As I will note at length in my chapter about word choice, William Strunk and E. B. White in *The Elements of Style* define a nonrestrictive clause as "one that does not serve to identify or define the antecedent noun.

> The audience, which had at first been indifferent, became more and more interested."

The clause "which had at first been indifferent" simply describes the general character of the audience. If the sentence had read "The audience that had at first been indifferent became more and more interested," the phrase "that had at first been indifferent" would restrict, would limit the identity of the audience—presumably in opposition to some other audience that had been interested from the beginning. That would make the clause restrictive. (*That* is always used for restrictive clauses and *which* for nonrestrictive clauses.) "Restrictive clauses," Strunk and White continue, "by contrast, are not parenthetic and are not set off by commas. Thus,

> People who live in glass houses shouldn't throw stones.

Here, the clause introduced by *who* does serve to tell which people are meant ..." Those who live in glass houses are meant, to the exclusion of people who don't. If the sentence had read "People, who live in glass houses, shouldn't throw stones," it would imply that everyone happens to live in glass houses; the clause "who live in glass houses" would merely describe the noun instead of identifying or defining it.

Sometimes only this pair of commas signifies whether a clause is restrictive or nonrestrictive, depending on what the writer intends. Lunsford and Connors comment,

> Notice how using or not using commas to set off such an element can change the meaning of a sentence.
>
>> The bus drivers rejecting the management offer remained on strike.
>> The bus drivers, rejecting the management offer, remained on strike.
>
> In the first sentence, not using commas to set off the phrase *rejecting the management offer* makes the clause restrictive, limiting the meaning of *The bus drivers*. This sentence says that only some of the total group of bus drivers—the ones who rejected the offer— remained on strike, implying that other drivers went back to work. In the second sentence, the commas around the clause make it nonrestrictive, implying that *The bus drivers* refers to all of the drivers and that all of them remained on strike.

If you have trouble figuring out if a clause is restrictive or nonrestrictive, Lunsford and Connors recommend that you "mentally delete the element, and then decide whether the deletion changes the meaning of the rest of the sentence or makes it unclear." In their second sample sentence, removing "rejecting the management offer" does not change the sentence's meaning or make it unclear. All the drivers are on strike, and therefore "rejecting the management offer" is not absolutely necessary to identify the subject. Removing the same clause from the first sample, however, does change its meaning: the clause indicates that only certain bus drivers remained on strike. Shortening the sentence to "The bus drivers remained on strike" misleads the reader into thinking all of them did.

"Now here's a funny thing," Truss relates. When this type of semi-parenthetical phrase "comes at the beginning or at the end, the grammatical rule of commas-in-pairs still applies, *even if you can only see one of them.* Thus:

Of course, there weren't enough tickets to go round.

is, from the grammatical point of view, the same as:

There weren't, of course, enough tickets to go round.

as well as:

There weren't enough tickets to go round, of course."

"Of course" doesn't really qualify as either restrictive or nonrestrictive, though; it fits more into the previous rule of setting off an interjection with a comma (or two, if it intrudes into the middle of the sentence, as in Truss's second example). Nonetheless, we can demonstrate the same point with Lunsford and Connors's sample sentences:

Rejecting the management offer, the bus drivers remained on strike.
The bus drivers remained on strike, rejecting the management offer.

The comma normally at the beginning or end of the nonrestrictive clause becomes "understood"—like *you* as the subject of a command—by virtue of the impossibility of placing it at the beginning or end of the sentence. It makes sense to place a nonrestrictive clause beginning with *which* at the end rather than at the beginning. Using *The Elements of Style*'s example, compare

The audience became more and more interested, which had at first been indifferent.

with

Which had at first been indifferent, the audience became more and more interested.

In the immortal words of Damon Wayans, "Homey don't play that."

In the professional writing I edit at work, nonrestrictive clauses in the middle of a sentence often lack their second commas. This mistake can only result from my co-workers not listening to the sentence as they write and not picking up on the phrase's semi-parenthetical nature, its status as a small enclave of language within the sentence. Truss maintains, "As with other paired bracketing devices (such as parentheses, dashes, and quotation marks), there is actual mental cruelty involved, incidentally, in opening up a pair of commas and then neglecting to deliver the closing one." When this happens, the writer frustrates the reader's expectation of completion and obscures where the main clause of the sentence resumes.

The last comma rule in the *Eats, Shoots and Leaves* list may be the most important: NEVER separate a noun from its verb with a comma. *The New St. Martin's Handbook* agrees, and adds that neither should we do so between a verb and its object or complement (the rest of the predicate) or between a preposition and its object. These grammatical elements rely on each other too much to function smoothly with an unnecessary interruption. I never cease to be surprised how many professionals would punctuate the last sentence this way:

These grammatical elements, rely on each other, too much to function smoothly with, an unnecessary interruption.

Orally, the comma represents a simple, brief pause. An emergency rule of thumb when you can't remember all of Lynne Truss's grammatical rules is to put one wherever you would pause in a sentence. Unfortunately, the fact that different people speak at different paces, some with more or fewer pauses than others, complicates this rule and surely contributes to the arguability over comma usage. One thing is certain: don't use too many commas in a single sentence. "A passage peppered with commas," Truss insists, "smacks simply of no backbone." A statement full of pauses sounds unsure and hesitant—like saying "um" over and over.

The semicolon primarily joins two separate sentences whose themes relate to each other so closely that you want them rolled into one. The proverb "Cowards die a thousand deaths; the brave die but once" displays the semicolon at its best. The semicolon looks like what it does: the upper point that looks like a period establishes the integrity of the first clause, or formally complete section, while the lower point that looks like a comma extends the sentence's meaning and the reader's attention to the second clause.

Truss defines the purpose of the semicolon in more specific detail: "... the main place for putting a semicolon ... is between two related sentences where there is no conjunction such as 'and' or 'but,' and where a comma would be ungrammatical ..." In other words, a semicolon replaces the comma splice mentioned before. Wienbroer et al. comment that certain transition words often follow the semicolon to clarify or delineate the relationship between the two clauses:

"however	therefore	otherwise
nevertheless	in other words	instead
for example	on the other hand	meanwhile
besides	furthermore	fortunately"

Additionally, they note that a comma comes after these words when they follow a semicolon. Writing a sentence like "Most Arabs are Muslims, however some are not," as many people I've edited for would, doesn't work because the comma implies that the second clause continues on a direct linear progression from the first, whereas *however* announces a shift in the sentence: the combination jars our sense of the sentence's meaning. A semicolon works better than a comma here because it marks a pivot in the sentence, allowing for what succeeds it to swing at an angle from what precedes it. Think of it as a hinge in the sentence. The ideas of the clauses on either side of it should be similar but not the same; otherwise, there would be no need for both. At the same time, a comma should follow *however* because of the pause necessary for the announcement of the different direction the sentence is about to take to sink in.

"There are times, however," Truss informs us, "when the semicolon is indispensable in another capacity: when it performs the duties of a kind of Special Policeman in the event of comma fights." It usually plays this more minor role by separating items in a list when one or more of the items contains a comma within it, as in "The napkins were pink; purple; and red, white, and blue." The semicolons make clear that there are three items, not five—two of the items are monochromatic and one consists of three colors.

The way the semicolon sounds reflects its structural function: a medium pause, longer than a comma but not as long as a period.

A colon signals that one part of a sentence introduces another. Strunk and White bid us, *"Use a colon after an independent clause to introduce a list of particulars, an appositive, an amplification, or an illustrative quotation."* They add, "It ... should not separate a verb from its complement or a preposition from its object." Thus, the following sentence they provide should have the colon it contains:

> "Your dedicated whittler requires three props: a knife, a piece of wood, and a back porch."

Another sentence they provide, however, does not need a colon:

> "Understanding is that penetrating quality of knowledge that grows from theory, practice, conviction, assertion, error, and humiliation."

A colon before this sentence's list would be superfluous; the preposition *from* already links it to the main body of the sentence. If you *really* wanted a colon in the sentence, you could recast it into something like "Understanding is that penetrating quality of knowledge that grows from several sources: theory, practice, conviction, assertion, error, and humiliation." Furthermore, Lunsford and Connors and Wienbroer et al. caution us against putting a colon after introductory verbs, prepositions, *such as*, *include* or *including*, *especially*, and forms of *to be*.

As the above two sentences indicate, the colon most frequently introduces lists. Probably its second most common use is to formally introduce quotes. But remember Strunk and White's remark that a colon preceding a quote must come after an independent clause—a grammatically complete sentence. One cannot write "Thomas Jefferson insisted that: 'All men are ... endowed by their Creator with certain inalienable rights ...'" *That*, as a preposition, tells the reader that more of one's own sentence remains to come; following it with a colon would just be another case of putting a colon after *from* in Strunk and White's second example sentence. Nor should one should write "Thomas Jefferson insisted: 'All men are ... endowed by their Creator with certain inalienable rights ...'" Elsewhere, *The Elements of Style* tells us, "A quotation grammatically in apposition or the direct object of a verb is preceded by a comma ..." (An appositive identifies or renames something before it; for example, this last quote identifies what my source "tells.") The quote itself is what Jefferson insisted, serving as the verb's direct object. As a result, the colon doesn't fly. To introduce this quote with a colon, one would have to write something like "Thomas Jefferson insisted on the intrinsic freedom of humanity: 'All men are ... endowed by their Creator with certain inalienable rights ...'" The writer provides the verb with a direct object of his or her own, which identifies what Jefferson insisted before we get to the quote. By the time we get to the colon, nothing but the quote needs to follow.

A complete sentence can come after a colon as well as before; Strunk and White write, "Join two independent clauses with a colon if the second interprets or amplifies the first.

> But even so, there was a directness and dispatch about animal burial: there was no stopover in the undertaker's foul parlor, no wreath or spray."

One could join these clauses with a semicolon, since their topics are linked. But the colon specifies how they are linked: it means that the second clause will explain why animal burial is direct. If the semicolon continues and refracts the path of the preceding clause, the colon broadens it.

More than any other punctuation mark, writers use the colon for effect. Lynne Truss notes that "in its simplest usage it rather theatrically announces what is to come"; she elaborates on this by citing two other writers. "H. W. Fowler said that the colon 'delivers the goods that have been invoiced in the preceding words' ..." Also, George Bernard Shaw wrote to T. E. Lawrence in response to the latter's request for literary advice, "When two statements are 'placed baldly in dramatic apposition,' ... use a colon." All this denotes that the colon is the climax of a thematic build-up before it, resulting in a release of thematic tension after it. The sentence my high school English teacher used as an example of the colon in action perfectly illustrates this tendency: when George C. Scott refused to accept an Oscar, he said, "I act for one reason, and one reason only: money." According to Truss, Shaw advised Lawrence to use a colon "also when you desire an abrupt 'pull-up' ..."

Consequently, colons usually take the form of a dramatic pause in speech. *Rules of Thumb for Business Writers* states, "Colons create suspense"; the listener could mentally fill its silence with a drum-roll. Because of this intentional feeling of leaving the reader or audience hanging, classically trained typists place two spaces between a colon and the next word, as though replicating on paper the sense of time stretching out as one waits for the colon to deliver what it heralds.

First and foremost concerning dashes, a dash is NOT the same as a hyphen. In the days of that old-time contraption the typewriter, a dash was typed as two hyphens "with no spaces before, between, or after," says *The New St. Martin's Handbook*. "In some software, a solid dash can be typed as it is.... In some computer programs, two typed hyphens are automatically converted into a solid dash." Truss relates, "... on my own Apple keyboard I have been for years discouraged ... by the belief that I had to make my own quasi-dashes from illicit double-taps on the hyphen. When I discovered a week ago that I could make a true dash by employing the alt key with the hyphen, it was truly one of the red-letter days of my life." In my experience, most word processing programs turn two hyphens into a dash. Excel does not.

What's a dash good for, then? It usually notes an additional thought after a sentence expresses its main idea: "A single dash sets off a comment or emphasizes material at the end of a sentence. It may also mark a sudden shift in tone, introduce a summary or explanation of what has come before," observes *The New St. Martin's Handbook*. *Rules of Thumb for Business Writers* says dashes "show an abrupt change of thought in midsentence, or connect a fragment to a sentence." The phrase after the dash usually tangentially or indirectly relates to the main idea, hence the feeling of suddenness or abruptness. *The Elements of Style* calls it an "interruption." *Eats, Shoots and Leaves* explains, "The word has identical roots with the verb 'to dash' (deriving from the Middle English verb *dasshen*, meaning 'to knock, to hurl, to break') and the point is that a single dash creates a dramatic disjunction which can be exploited for humor, for bathos, for shock." Truss suggests that it "can act as a bridge between bits of fractured sense."

The dash lends a degree of informality to writing. Truss writes that "it enhances conversational tone," reflecting the choppy, staccato rhythm of speech. This very quality makes it dangerous to overuse. Conversation is often choppy because it's sloppy. Lunsford and Connors warn, "In fact, you should use dashes very carefully ... because too many of them create a jerky, disconnected effect that makes it hard for readers to follow your thought." After all, because they're used for fragments, a lot of dashes can imply a lot of loose connections between thoughts. Wienbroer et al. note, "However—handy though they are—too many can make it seem as if you've dashed off your report." Pun intended.

Occasionally, one of these fragments or tangents gets plunked right into the middle of a sentence instead of at the end. Set it off with a dash before it and a dash after it: "She brought all her sweaters with her—even though it was summer—on her Florida vacation." The dashes set the phrase apart from the rest of the sentence for emphasis, to show its importance.
Given the dash's nature, it should come as no surprise that we usually speak it as a sharp pause. Usually, the first stressed syllable after the dash is spoken more loudly. Say the following sentence to yourself and you'll know what I mean: "He walked into the snowstorm in his boxer shorts—who knows why."

Parentheses enclose a phrase to show it is less important, incidental, to the rest of the sentence. Truss explains that the material within parentheses usually serves "to add information, to clarify, to explain, to illustrate ..." The parentheses in "Most deep-sea fish (like tuna or cod) are large" tell us that the writer focuses less on the specific fish he or she mentions than on the category; the writer mentions tuna and cod solely to allow the reader to relate to the category. Enclosing a phrase in parentheses essentially achieves the opposite of enclosing it with dashes. In fact, Lynne Truss writes, "But as they sit on the page, it seems to me brackets [British for "parentheses"] half-remove the intruding aside, half-suppress it; while the dashes warmly welcome it in, with open arms."

A whole sentence may be put in parentheses if the writer wants to inject a complete thought as an aside to the preceding sentence. For instance, at the end of the last paragraph, I could have written "(Don't ask me why she has a semicolon in this sentence.)." At the same time, one shouldn't have a lot of text inside parentheses. As with paired commas, "there is a certain amount of anxiety created once a bracket has been opened that is not dissipated until it's bloody well closed again," Truss writes.

We usually signal words in parentheses by speaking them in a slightly lower tone, with a quick pause before. Parentheses should not be confused with brackets (which the British call "square brackets"), "an editor's way of clarifying the meaning of a direct quote without actually changing any of the words" by inserting explanatory text or missing parts of speech. I did this in the first paragraph of this section with the phrase "[British for 'parentheses']" to explain Lynne Truss's use of the word "brackets."

Ellipses (...) represent words a writer has intentionally left out of a direct quote—usually because they are not immediately relevant to the subject at hand, or perhaps to make the quote more grammatical. One can also use them at the end of one's own sentence to "trail off in an intriguing manner," writes Truss. She invokes "the power of erotic suggestion contained in the traditional three-dot chapter ending ('He swept her into his arms. She was powerless to resist. All she knew was, she loved him ...') ..." Used frequently for this purpose, they can become extremely tedious. Truss comments that ellipses are "turning up increasingly in emails as shorthand for 'more to come, actually ... it might be related to what I've just written ... but the main thing is I haven't finished ... let's just wait and see ... I could go on like this for hours.'" Final ellipses indicate an incomplete thought or an idea left to the imagination; rarely is there room for that in information-driven professional writing.

Ellipses mirror how the voice trails off into an elongated pause when leaving a spoken sentence incomplete. If the words replaced by the ellipses come immediately after the end of a complete sentence in the quote, type the preceding sentence's period, then the ellipses.

We all know a hyphen joins two words when they function as a compound word. Kingsley Amis, in *The King's English*, examines when two words need to be joined. "The hyphen is properly and necessarily used to join the halves of a two-word adjectival phrase," he writes, such as *run-down*, and continues, "Hyphens are also required when a phrase of more than two words is used adjectivally ..." *Out-of-pocket expenses* is such a phrase. Adjectival phrases consisting of an adverb not ending in *-ly* plus an adjective require hyphens, he notes; a *well-designed* program is not the same as a *well designed* program, a planned program free from illness. These combinations should not have a hyphen, however, when the adverb ends in *-ly*, as in "thickly crusted ice." Additionally, Amis declares, "The commonest fault in the use of the hyphen, and the hardest to eradicate, is found when an adjectival phrase is used predicatively," or after the verb of the noun it describes. "So a gent may write of a *hard-to-conquer* mountain peak but not of a mountain peak that remains *hard-to-conquer*, an *often-proposed* solution but not of one that is *often-proposed*." If the modifying phrase comes after the verb of the noun it modifies, leave the hyphen out.

Eats, Shoots and Leaves adds, "Certain prefixes traditionally require hyphens: un-American, anti-Apartheid, pro-hyphens, quasi-grammatical." But keep in mind that there are words that these prefixes are written as part of, like *unable* or *antifreeze*. These are commonly used words, with long histories, that you'll find in most dictionaries. Words with hyphenated prefixes tend to be neologisms coined in the recent past or for a particular occasion, some of which have found their way into habitual use. Some words have hyphenated prefixes to differentiate them from an entirely separate word with the same prefix and same root word written together. *The New St. Martin's Handbook* explains, "*Re-cover* means 'cover again'; the hyphen distinguishes it from *recover*, meaning 'get well.'"

Also, writes Truss, "Purely for expediency, the hyphen is used to prevent an unpleasant linguistic condition called 'letter collision.' However much you might want to create compound words, there will always be some ghastly results, such as 'deice' (de-ice) or 'shelllike' (shell-like)." The hyphen helps the first example phonetically, ensuring that the *e* and *i* are pronounced separately; it helps the second example graphically, preventing an unheard-of triple succession of the same letter. Truss concludes, "When a hyphenated phrase is coming up, and you are qualifying it beforehand, it is necessary to write, 'He was a two- or three-year-old.'"

With such a plethora of rules to keep straight, why don't we just get rid of the hyphen? A great many professionals already do in their writing, whether out of laziness, willfulness, or illiteracy. Believe it or not, even the tiny hyphen contributes mightily to directing how we read. In the adjectival phrases that Truss and Amis give us rules for, the hyphen ties the first modifier to the second modifier instead of to the noun. Failing to shift the relationship of these words with one another when necessary using a hyphen can result in hilarity. As Truss argues, "Those much-invoked examples of the little used car, the superfluous hair remover, the pickled herring merchant, the slow moving traffic and the two hundred odd members of the Conservative Party would all be lost without it."

Quotation marks don't pose many problems in and of themselves. We use them when citing someone else's exact words. As *The New St. Martin's Handbook* reminds us, we should not use them when paraphrasing or summarizing what someone else said or wrote in our own words.

Lunsford and Connors also note the customary guideline for long quotes: "If the passage you wish to quote exceeds four typed lines, set it off from the rest of the text by starting it on a new line and indenting each line ten spaces from the left margin. This format, known as block quotation, does not require quotation marks." Personally, I indent block quotations only one tab length in from the margin, which varies in the number of character spaces depending on the font I use. Unless the publication's style guide demands otherwise, I also type block quotations in a slightly smaller size than my own text to further set them off—if my essay or article is in 12-point, I type the block quotation in 10-point. In magazines and books, block quotations are usually printed in a smaller typeface.

The effect of quotation marks on other punctuation marks creates more difficulty. We've already dealt with introducing quotes in the comma and colon sections. "When a piece of dialogue is attributed at its end, conclude it with a comma inside the inverted commas [what the British call quotation marks]," writes Truss.

Regarding other punctuation dynamics caused by quotation marks, Truss refers to "American grammarians insisting that, if a sentence ends with a phrase in inverted commas, all the terminal punctuation marks for the sentence must come tidily inside the speech marks, even when this doesn't seem to make sense." I've observed a more nuanced practice. Periods and commas always go inside closing quotation marks. Truss argues, "When only a fragment of speech is being quoted, put punctuation outside the inverted commas ..." I don't know if this is accepted usage in Great Britain, but I've never seen it. On the contrary, opening a book a friend lent me entitled *Home Comforts*, by Cheryl Mendelsohn, I found this random example: "Many home dryers now also offer 'electronic drying,' in which the machine automatically senses the moisture level and turns off ..." The comma is not integral to the referenced phrase "electronic drying," yet the comma is placed inside the quotation marks just as it would be for attributing a direct quote afterwards, for consistency's and simplicity's sake.

The New St. Martin's Handbook notes, "Question marks, exclamation points, and dashes go *inside* closing quotation marks if they are part of the quotation, *outside* if they are not." If you ask the question, put the question mark after; if your source asks the question, put the question mark before. (I can't imagine when a quote would end with a dash. Replace that dash with ellipses to show that your source's sentence continues beyond where you end the quote.) If, however, you want your quote to end an independent clause followed by a colon or a semicolon, place the colon or semicolon outside the quotation marks. In these cases, this makes clear that you, not your source, are joining your source's words and thoughts with those to come.

Lunsford and Connors mention that quotation marks also highlight words or phrases invented by the writer, or indicate that the writer uses the terms within them ironically. Someone like myself who hates the government of Communist China might refer to it snidely in writing as the "People's" Republic; it's like prefacing the term with "so-called". Quotation marks also enclose the titles of short creative works or subordinate parts of large creative works: short stories, brief poems, essays, newspaper or magazine articles, chapters of books, songs, and so forth.

One usage of quotation marks does famously differ on opposite sides of the Atlantic. For a quote within a quote, we Americans enclose it in single quotation marks—typed as an apostrophe—within the larger quote enclosed in double quotation marks. I've done this in various quotes throughout the article. The British use single quotation marks for ordinary quotations and double quotation marks for quotes within quotes.

Technically, italics may not qualify as punctuation, but they are similar and important enough to mention. Truss enumerates four uses for italics. First, for the titles of major creative works such as books; record albums and works of classical music such as symphonies, sonatas, and operas; plays; movies; and works of graphic art. Names of periodicals also take italics. Second, italics emphasize words that the writer wants to call attention to—usually because he or she finds them or what they express shocking, alarming, or strange. Foreign words and phrases are italicized, as well as words the writer refers to when writing about language.

Italics also indicate internal dialogue, what someone thinks to himself or herself without speaking aloud. This technique comes into play more in creative writing, and the vast majority of professional writing will present little opportunity or need for it.

Along with the metaphors for punctuation presented in the beginning of the article, Lynne Truss relates in *Eats, Shoots and Leaves* that she encountered a writer who "tells us that punctuation marks are the traffic signals of language: they tell us when to slow down, notice this, take a detour, and stop." This metaphor strikes me as the most fitting description of punctuation's purpose: it tells the reader how to conduct himself or herself through what he or she reads. Consider Biblical Hebrew's lack of internal punctuation. While the system of cantillation marks for public reading of the Bible in Hebrew in some respects makes up for this lack, the solitary reader unfamiliar with this system might be hard-pressed to understand the Scriptures in the original as phrase runs headlong into phrase within a single verse.

Without punctuation, your readers might find themselves in the same predicament. You can't deliver your work aloud to every reader you have; they can't all have the interpretive benefit of the inflection of your voice, to say nothing of body language. Proper punctuation gives your reader a smooth drive through your prose, preventing it from devolving into a linguistic free-for-all and ending up in a crumpled heap—in your reader's wastebasket.

WORD CHOICE, COMMUNICATION, AND SELF-PRESENTATION

All you professional ladies out there: could you imagine giving a presentation to a top client while dressed in a white blouse, a sharp blazer in your favorite color—and Daisy Dukes? And professional men, can you see yourself arriving for a job interview wearing dress pants, a button-down dress shirt, a necktie—and a jean jacket? (Pretend, for convenience's sake, that footwear is optional.)

We both know what the answer is, but I'll be tedious and state it anyway. Of course not. Yet many professionals commit the linguistic equivalent of the fashion tragedies described above in their writing: poor word choice. Like a discordant ensemble of clothes, bad diction in professional writing can make one look like a fool without enough common sense to distinguish differences in things or to ensure consistency in what he or she does.

Frequently confused words probably present the easiest place to start for the lexically challenged—as well as the easiest element of faulty word choice to correct, provided the writer cares. Below are some of the most common verbal mix-ups I've encountered. This first group consists of words that sound similar.

Affect and Effect. Quite easy, really, in their most common sense of "to influence" or "an outcome": *affect* is the verb and *effect* is the noun. Both words do have secondary meanings as the opposite part of speech. Bill Bryson notes in *Bryson's Dictionary of Troublesome Words*, "*Effect* as a verb means to accomplish ('The prisoners effected an escape')." This usage, however, has grown unbearably trite with time; no one should write a sentence like Bryson's example when they can write "The prisoners escaped" or, at most, "The prisoners managed to escape." "*Affect* as a noun," he continues, "has a narrow psychological meaning to do with emotional states." In other words, it's psychobabble for "emotion."

Complement and Compliment. The first word means to work well together with something or someone, as in making up for its or one's flaws. It's a shorter way of saying "completement." The second word has to do with giving someone props. A well-matched husband and wife *complement* each other; a polite guest *compliments* his host on her cooking.

Continual and Continuous. Not just two different words for the same thing, as Bill Bryson reveals:

> *Continual* refers to things that happen repeatedly but not constantly. *Continuous* indicates an uninterrupted sequence. However, few readers will be aware of this distinction, and the writer who requires absolute clarity will generally be better advised to use *incessant* or *uninterrupted* for continuous and *intermittent* for continual.

Discreet and Discrete. The former means confidential, between you and me—not public information. The latter means separate, clearly distinct. *Discrete* usually refers to units comprising a larger entity. It comes from the same root as *accrete* and *secrete*; it might help to remember that *discreet* is like *secret* and *discrete* is like *secrete*. O.K., maybe that doesn't help.

Enormity and Enormousness. Among the fastest growing misuses in America today. The late British novelist Kingsley Amis complains in his book *The King's English*, "... when Eliot (T. S.) wrote of 'the *enormity* of man's ignorance' he was just getting it wrong: by rights he should have written *enormousness*." Both words come from the same Latin root, as Amis tells us: "*ex-* or *e-* = out of, *norma* = norm, the ordinary ..." But *The Elements of Style* bids us regarding *enormity*: "Use only in the sense of 'monstrous wickedness.' Misleading, if not wrong, when used to express bigness." Thus, *enormity* pertains to morality and *enormousness* to size. This means that if T. S. Eliot argued that man's ignorance is his own fault, Eliot's choice would be correct and Amis wrong.

Farther and Further. Unlike *discreet* and *discrete*, these two words are rapidly becoming interchangeable in common usage. Like the previous pair, however, authorities still uphold their distinct meanings. They agree that *farther* should be used only for literal physical distance: "Washington, D.C. is 400 miles farther away than New York." William Strunk and E. B. White's *The Elements of Style* says to use "*further* as a time or quantity word"; *Bryson's Dictionary of Troublesome Words* advises to use "*further* in contexts involving figurative distance ('I can take this plan no further')." In short, use *further* for anything besides literal physical space.

Forego and Forgo. This one elicits the most sympathy from me, though I'm not sure why. As Bryson lays it out, "*Forego* means to go before," (see how it's spelled?) "to precede. To do without is to *forgo*." For *forgo*, think of it having the same prefix as *forswear*, to renounce or give something up.

Gambit and Gamble. Probably because they sound similar, many people use *gambit* to mean *gamble*—or, at the most specific, to mean a ploy, a strategic move designed to provoke response. "Properly," as Bill Bryson tells us and as any chess enthusiast could, "a gambit is an opening move that involves some strategic sacrifice or concession."

Home and Hone. To *hone in* on something does not mean to concentrate one's focus on it. In fact, it means nothing at all. As *Bryson's Dictionary of Troublesome Words* indicates, *hone* means "to sharpen, as in honing a knife . . ." To concentrate one's focus on something is to *home in*, taken from fighter pilot parlance for zeroing in on a target. Come to think of it, *zero in* is probably easier to remember; I've never heard anyone say they were "threeing in" on something.

Lay and Lie. These two verbs constitute a veritable boogeyman for many writers. The problem lies (not "lays") with *lay* being the past tense form of *lie*. How to keep them straight? Strunk and White explain that "lay" is a transitive verb, an action that one always does to something else. It must have a direct object. Its present, past, past participle, and present participle forms, respectively, are *lay, laid, laid, laying*. As usual, Bill Bryson offers helpful example sentences illustrating these forms in use:

PRESENT: "I lay the book on the table."
PAST: "Yesterday I laid the book on the table."
PRESENT PERFECT: "I have already laid the book on the table."
Here are some examples of my own of other tenses, following Bryson's pattern:
PAST PERFECT: I had laid the book on the table before yesterday.
PAST PROGRESSIVE: I was laying the book on the table every day for a week.
PRESENT PROGRESSIVE: I am laying the book on the table.

Lie is an intransitive verb, an action one only does to oneself. It takes no direct object; nothing else immediately receives the action. Its present, past, past participle, and present participle, as listed by Strunk and White, are *lie, lay, lain, lying*. Here are Bill Bryson's sample sentences:

PRESENT: "I lie down; I am laying down." (Actually, this last one is present progressive, but hey, that's one less example I have to make up.)
PAST: "Last night I lay down to sleep."
PRESENT PERFECT: "I have lain in bed all day."
And mine, for other tenses:
PAST PERFECT: I had lain in bed a long time last Sunday before falling asleep.
PAST PROGRESSIVE: I was lying in bed all that week.

Principal and Principle. This pair annoys me the most when they're misused, because I agree with Kingsley Amis in *The King's English* that this mostly happens out of "[l]aziness." They do come from the same root meaning "first," "most important." *Principal* is the adjective; it shares the *–al* suffix with hundreds of other adjectives. *Principle* is the noun, meaning "a fundamental value." Perhaps the meaning of this form can be remembered because the form shares its final three letters with *scruple*, another kind of moral or behavioral guideline. Some may say, "What about a school principal? That's the *–al* form used as a noun." True, but it's still an adjectival form; it could be shorthand for "principal officer" or something like that. (For that matter, *president* is actually an adjective, a funny alternative gerund for *presiding*.)

A few months ago I received a campaign mailing from a mayoral candidate that discussed improving public schools "Real reform," it read, "will include giving principles, teachers, and parents more autonomy …" No wonder he's worried about education.

Prescribe and Proscribe. Though they differ by merely one letter, these two words are essentially antonyms. A prescription is something our doctors write to allow us to receive medicine. Don't confuse this with *proscription*, a prohibition. Remember this by the common prefix in both *proscribe* and *prohibit*.

Stationary and Stationery. At a bookstore where I used to work, the writing supplies section was labeled with a sign reading "STATIONARY." As a writer, it was one of the most mortifying experiences of my life: *stationary* means motionless. Fine writing paper is *stationery*. As you might guess, we never rearranged that section's merchandise.

Here's another category of frequently confused words: words whose meanings are somewhat similar, but not exactly enough to be interchangeable.

Aggravate and Irritate. One of the most common mistakes of this kind. As *The Elements of Style* points out, "The first means 'to add to' an already troublesome or vexing matter or condition." Literally, it means to make more grave. "The second means 'to vex' or 'to annoy' or 'to chafe.'" Bryson sharply observes, "People can never be aggravated, only circumstances."

Dialogue and Discussion. Kingsley Amis reminds us that, strictly speaking, a *dialogue* is a conversation between only two people, because of the same Greek prefix meaning "two" used in the term "carbon dioxide" (CO_2), for example. A *discussion* can have any number of participants. One could argue that Plato's dialogues have several characters, but usually Socrates is talking with only one other person at a time.

Disinterested and Uninterested. Kingsley Amis proclaims this the "most famous and ancient of all misuses and not for that reason any less a case of ignorant bullshit." *Uninterested* means taking no interest, bored. The word and its definition are simple enough, yet people persist in putting *disinterested*, meaning unbiased or impartial—having no vested interest—in its place. If you were on trial for murder, you would want a disinterested jury to hear your case; you would NOT want an uninterested jury.

Amis adds that "by a process not altogether unique, the misuse has acquired a shade of meaning all its own. Thus a schoolboy who is uninterested in the lesson will merely be sunk in mindless apathy and gloom, whereas his *disinterested* classmate will be pulling faces and launching paper aeroplanes, actively expressing boredom." I haven't encountered this usage. I just wonder how long it will take for either or both terms to be applied to checking accounts.

Imply and Infer. A speaker or writer *implies* something when suggesting it while leaving it unstated. The audience *infers* this unstated meaning by reading (or listening) between the lines. *The King's English* says, "I imply, you infer."

Less and Fewer. "*Less* refers to [general] quantity, fewer to number," declare Strunk and White. *Fewer* applies to items that can be counted in individual units, like pears, napkins, or golf caddies. *Less* refers to things that are not composed of separate countable objects, like time, gasoline, or stupidity. Bryson elaborates:

> A rougher but more useful guide is to use *less* with singular nouns (less money, less sugar) and *fewer* with plural nouns (fewer houses, fewer doctors).... An apparent exception to the rule can be seen here: "... but some people earn fewer than $750 a year" (*Times*). Although $750 is inarguably a plural sum, it functions as a singular. We see it as a totality, not as a collection of individual dollars. Thus the sentence should read "less than $750."

It's simply a more specific way of saying "less money."

Like and As. Interchangeable in colloquial English, *like* and *as* do not have the same function; complications arise because they each have two functions, which I'll call descriptive and identifying. In their descriptive function, the words indicate *how* something is or is done—they relate to quality. *The Elements of Style* says, "*Like* governs nouns and pronouns; before phrases and clauses the equivalent word is *as*." The poet Elizabeth Bishop was always dismayed that her creative writing students at Harvard couldn't find the error in the old cigarette slogan "Winston tastes good like a cigarette should." According to Strunk and White's rule, since the prepositional phrase in question contains both a noun and its verb, the sentence should read: "Winston tastes good, as a cigarette should." *Like* would be used if the prepositional phrase had no verb and the sentence simply compared Winston to another brand, as in "Winston tastes good, like Benson & Hedges." "On the face of it," Bill Bryson surmises, "the rule is simple: *as* and *as if* are always followed by a verb; *like* never is." Ever sensitive to complications, though, he announces: "There is also one apparent inconsistency in the rule, in that *like* may be used when it comes between *feel* and an *–ing* verb: 'He felt like walking'; 'I feel like going abroad this year.'" But this is an idiomatic use outside its normal function of comparing.

Like and *as* perform their second, identifying function when used in similes. Their relationship to verbs stays the same as in the descriptive function: we would say, "She runs like a cheetah" but "She runs as a cheetah does." *As*, however, has its fair share of exceptions. For one, it also plays a more strictly identifying—and not comparative—role. I could say, "I'm writing this article as someone with experience in professional writing." I'm not writing it "like" someone with experience in professional writing; I AM one. Therefore, *as* serves to define me. When doubled, it plays a more comparative and less strictly identifying role: "She runs as swiftly as a cheetah." In both these exceptions, no verb follows *as*.

38

May and Might. Although even I mix them up in speaking, they're one of the easiest pairs to use correctly when making the effort to do so. As noted in *The King's English*, *may* signifies permission and *might* signifies uncertain possibility. It might rain tomorrow; if it does, the rain won't ask us if it's OK beforehand.

Oral and Verbal. This misuse has become so rampant that fighting its infiltration into standard usage may be a lost cause. *Bryson's Dictionary of Troublesome Words* tells us that, due to its original Latin meaning, *verbal* really pertains to anything having to do with words. When most people talk about a "verbal agreement," they really mean *oral*—spoken, as opposed to written. The legal profession upholds this distinction in the term "oral contract."

Shall and Will. These verbs tend not to cause error so much as unnecessary confusion; just a few weeks ago, the ESL student I tutor asked me about the difference between them. According to Bryson,

> The rule most frequently propounded is that to express simple futurity you should use *shall* in the first person and *will* in the second and third persons, and to express determination (or volition) you should do the reverse. But by that rule Churchill blundered grammatically when he vowed, "We shall fight in the fields and in the streets, we shall fight in the hills; we shall never surrender." As did MacArthur when he said at Corregidor, "I shall return." As have all those who have ever sung "We Shall Overcome."
>
> The simple fact is that whether you use *shall* or *will* in a given instance depends very much on your age and your birthplace and the emphasis with which you mean to express yourself.

An even simpler fact is that hardly anyone says *shall* anymore; it feels archaic and hoity-toity. Forget about it. If you ask me, nothing could better express determination or volition than *will*.

That and Which. "*That* is the defining, or restrictive, pronoun, *which* the nondefining, or nonrestrictive," say Strunk and White. So what the heck does that mean? In the sentence "The article that I am writing is about word choice," the phrase "that I am writing" specifies and identifies the article. But if I change the sentence to "The article, which I am writing, is about word choice," the phrase "which I am writing" is incidental, semiparenthetical (and hence is set off by commas); the fact that I am writing the article is subordinate to the fact that it is about word choice. Put simply, use *that* when you want to emphasize what follows and *which* when what follows isn't quite as important as the rest of the sentence.

Amis comments, "The problem is often duckable by omitting any pronoun and writing 'the book I was reading' . . ." However, this only really works for *that*. "The book I was reading" still restricts, defines, identifies the book. Only by inserting *which* and a pair of commas can we say in a lower tone, "It just so happens that I was in the process of reading it."

Another class of diction snares are words that writers tend to use incorrectly or inappropriately, without confusing them with any other word.

Absolutely. "This adverb means 'completely' or 'entirely.' Take care that the word is not used loosely to mean 'very,'" writes Arthur H. Bell in *NTC's Business Writer's Handbook*. For example, if I am *absolutely* tired, I am incapable of anything but falling asleep.

Comparatively. This word means exactly what it says. "'Comparatively little progress was made in the talks yesterday' (*Guardian*). Compared with what?" Bryson demands. *Comparatively* is not a mitigating or qualifying modifier like *somewhat*, nor should it be used in the sense of "for this particular situation." Only use it when relating your subject to something else.

Compendium. Bryson writes that "the word is often taken to mean vast and all-encompassing. In fact, a compendium is a succinct summary or abridgement."

Compound. As a verb, Bryson states, it means to combine—it should not be used to mean to increase or to intensify. Compound interest isn't just "extra" interest. It's interest assessed on old unpaid interest as well as on the principal; the principal and the old interest are combined into a single outstanding sum from which to calculate interest.

Condone. I once saw Ice T on *Late Night With Conan O'Brien* talking about an album that, if I remember correctly, he produced, in which pimps told their stories backed by music (without explaining why anyone would want to hear that). In conclusion, Ice T said of their occupation, "I'm not condoning it ..." He probably used *condone* incorrectly. "It means to pardon, forgive, overlook," Bill Bryson writes. "You can condone an action without supporting it."

Stalemate. To continue the chess theme introduced with *gambit*, Bill Bryson reproves those who talk or write about "ending the stalemate": "Stalemates don't end. A chess match that reaches stalemate is not awaiting a more decisive outcome; the stalemate *is* the outcome." In chess, a stalemate occurs when no more legal moves are possible. Those using *stalemate* improperly should use *deadlock* instead.

Still other types of improper word use exist. Recent history has seen a curious phenomenon in English: the coinage of words that make no sense because they are internally redundant. *Bryson's Dictionary of Troublesome Words* cites a perfect example: "'In almost every other regard the two are coequal' (*Guardian*). A generally fatuous term. *Co-* adds nothing to *equal* that *equal* doesn't already say alone." Another word—although, as Bryson notes, it's not even a real word—meaning the opposite of the way it's used is that old stand-by of improper English, *irregardless*. It's internally redundant because it's a one-word double negative: "without no regard."

A similar plague of word choice is mixed metaphors. Andrea Lunsford and Robert Connors write in *The New St. Martin's Handbook*, "Mixed metaphors are comparisons that are not consistent. Instead of creating a clear and dominant impression, they confuse the reader by pulling against one another, often in unintentionally funny ways." When I was a graduate student, I once complained to my creative writing professor about a long spell without publishing, "I've been striking out lately, which I know is par for the course"—joining terminology from two very different sports. Mixed metaphors tend to indicate that the writer ignores detail and has trouble grasping the differences among categories.

Certain words are often used unnecessarily. Before discussing specific examples, I should state two general principles on this topic. First, as *The Elements of Style* advises, "Save the auxiliaries *would, should, could, may, might,* and *can* for situations involving real uncertainty." Readers, especially of business writing, don't like a hesitant writer who always qualifies his or her statements. Qualification is a sign of lack of confidence; lack of confidence is a sign of incompetence. Second, use as few words as possible to convey your whole meaning.

The Elements of Style likens overloaded diction to fatty food: "Rich, ornate prose is hard to digest, generally unwholesome, and sometimes nauseating."

A reason why some words are used unnecessarily is that they are inherently superfluous. Trust Bill Bryson to go for the jugular on *activity*, one of the most notorious culprits: "Often a sign of prolixity, as here: 'The warnings followed a week of earthquake activity throughout the region' (*Independent*). Just make it 'a week of earthquakes.'" *Activity* is an empty noun that forces a full noun like *earthquake* to become an adjective. A similar dynamic occurs with *basis* in this example from Bryson: "'Det. Chief Supt. Peter Tapping ... said he would review the search on a day-to-day basis' (*Independent*). Why not make it 'would review the search daily' and save five words?" In this case, *basis* as an empty noun prevents the rather flat adjective *day-to-day* from becoming a full adverb, *daily*, modifying a full verb, *review*. The same applies to *area, character, field*, and *situation*, listed by Lunsford and Connors as "empty words" that "are so general and so overused that they contribute no real meaning to a sentence."

Generally, one should closely consider modifiers for removal when revising one's writing to make it more concise. "Write with nouns and verbs, not with adjectives and adverbs," counsels *The Elements of Style*. I remember my Advanced Composition instructor in college telling us why the novelist John Fowles was his favorite writer: "He doesn't use any adjectives." That made his writing stronger, he said—more vigorous. The first such modifier to go should be *very*. If you've ever seen the movie *Dead Poets Society*, you may remember Robin Williams's character instilling this principle in his students: "A person is not *very sad*, he is ... *morose*." Why make two words, an empty modifier and a flat noun or verb, do what one full noun or verb can do better? *The Elements of Style* reiterates, "*Rather, very, little, pretty*—these are the leeches that infect the pond of prose, sucking the blood of words."

Other modifiers can also be tiresomely empty. Case in point, thanks to Bryson: "'Last week, twenty-five years after it was first conceived ...' (*Time*). Delete *first*. Something can be conceived only once." He also gives us a piece of his mind about *different*: "Often used unnecessarily, sometimes by the most careful of writers: 'This manifested itself in countless different ways' (Daniel J. Boorstin, *Cleopatra's Nose*)." Since the ways are countless, it stands to reason they are not all the same.

Some words are unnecessary because other words in the sentence render them redundant. Chief among these is *not* when combined with a negative word to state a positive condition; for example, "a not unfriendly gesture" instead of "a friendly gesture." Double negatives are stylistic taboos as well as grammatical errors. They're too contrived, too precious, too oblique— and therefore call too much attention to the writer's style and away from the writer's subject. "Make definite assertions," Strunk and White teach. "Use the word *not* as a means of denial or antithesis, never as a means of evasion."

Other unnecessary words stem from stock phrases we tend to use because when we converse our brains are often on auto-pilot; when we write our brains should be on auto-pilot only for notes or for the rough draft, if ever. As with the individual words we covered, some stock phrases are simply superfluous. *The King's English* identifies "the question as to whether" as a prime example. The word "whether" itself denotes uncertainty; adding the rest of the phrase is like saying, "The issue of the subject ..." Furthermore, *Bryson's Dictionary of Troublesome Words* observes, "In nearly every instance, removing *in order* [as in "in order to"] tightens the sentence without altering the sense." Lunsford and Connors comment on the absurdity of "saying that something is large *in size* or red *in color* or that two ingredients should be mixed *together*." Also like individual unnecessary words, some stock phrases are redundant. The redundancy of many should be obvious if we are careful about language, such as "added bonus" (Amis), "close proximity," and "general consensus" (Bryson). A few redundancies are more subtle or esoteric. "Even the most careful users of English frequently, but unnecessarily, refer to an 'old adage.' An adage is by definition old," writes Bryson. He also notes, "'In greater London' or 'in the London area' says the same thing as 'in the greater London area,' but says it more simply."

Poor word choice can damage a writer's credibility and readability. Using words improperly or confusedly can make one a laughingstock in the manner of Norm Crosby, the comedian who bases his act on purposefully saying the wrong words—like *stagnant* in place of *pregnant* and *incognito* in place of *unconscious*. Sloppy diction can make your thinking seem sloppy, and an audience of managers and clients might infer that your actions are equally sloppy. Using unnecessary words could make the information you intend to convey seem buried under a layer of fluff like the cotton wadding stuffed into medicine bottles, and leave your audience suspicious of why your message needs so much buffering.

Writing reflects on the writer. Don't let your writing look as if you wrote it first thing in the morning after rolling out of bed. Trim it, clean it up, and put your best face forward.

STYLE IN PROFESSIONAL WRITING

In the previous chapter I discussed word choice, a major factor in establishing a writer's style—the manner in which a writer uses language. To a great extent style is a personal and individual matter, like the way one parts one's hair. Still, some approaches to using language in writing succeed more than others, and some basic principles exist that allow us to distinguish between, and note what contributes to, ineffective and effective prose style.

Style shouldn't be set in stone. You'll probably have to adapt your style to various types of writing performed for various purposes. For persuasive writing one would use an impassioned, but not flamboyant, style; a calm, yet not dull or mechanical, style better suits expository writing. Choosing words appropriate to the task at hand plays the most essential part in effective style. As Lunsford and Connors illustrate, "One restaurant's 'down-home beef stew' may look and taste much like another's 'boeuf bourguignonne,' but in each case the choice of language aims to say something not only about the food but also about the restaurant serving it."

The tone in which the writer addresses the reader comprises another fundamental aspect of style. In *Rules of Thumb for Business Writers*, Diana Roberts Wienbroer et al. advise, "Good writing has the feel of a real person talking—warm, natural, and direct. Excessive formality makes your writing stilted and difficult to read." Lunsford and Connors tell us to beware of pompous language. "Pompous language is unnecessarily formal for the purpose, audience, or topic," they write. "Hence it often gives writing an insincere or unintentionally humorous tone, making the writer's idea seem less significant or believable." This fault causes the downfall of many inexpert writers who try to impress their readers by loading their writing with the most arcane and most Latinate words they can. They shoot high by straining after an elevated tone; too often they use words improperly, and their shot falls to the ground short of their target. "Avoid the elaborate, the pretentious, the coy, and the cute," advises *The Elements of Style*. "Do not be tempted by a twenty-dollar word when there is a ten-center handy, ready and able. Anglo-Saxon is a livelier tongue than Latin, so use Anglo-Saxon words."

At the same time, *Rules of Thumb for Business Writers* tells us, "this doesn't mean that you should use slang, sarcasm, or little jokes." Lunsford and Connors assert, "For most academic and professional writing, however, more formal language is appropriate because you are addressing people you do not know well." *The Elements of Style* asserts, "... *gut* is a lustier noun than *intestine*, but the two words are not interchangeable, because *gut* is often inappropriate, being too coarse for the context." Stay buttoned up, but down to earth.

Three major flaws contribute to poor style: weakness, imprecision, and vagueness or abstraction. What makes writing weak? The excessive Latinization mentioned by *The Elements of Style* above is a major factor. Since, as it says, "Anglo-Saxon is a livelier tongue than Latin," writing that turns away from simple Anglo-Saxon vocabulary time and again will tend to sound as dead as the Latin language itself. No valid reason exists under any circumstance to choose *utilize* over *use*; no one would ever say to his or her partner on a date, "Pardon me while I utilize the bathroom."

I should make a note here about jargon, "the special vocabulary of a trade or profession, enabling members to speak and write concisely to one another," as *The New St. Martin's Handbook* explains. An example of jargon is *patella*, the medical name for the kneecap. Professional writing often deals with subjects that carry a good deal of their own jargon with them; however, Lunsford and Connors warn, "It should be reserved as much as possible for a specific technical audience." An abundance of jargon in writing can feel alienating and irrelevant to a general audience that does not regularly use such jargon themselves. Therefore, only health care professionals should use *patella* instead of *kneecap*, and preferably only when speaking or writing to other health care professionals. If your audience has the same level of technical knowledge about your subject as you do, says *Rules of Thumb for Business Writers*, "technical knowledge has its rightful place. It can save time and effort because it is instantly recognizable by the people within that field." Otherwise, "strive to use everyday words as often as possible." If you find the advantage of brevity in using jargon outweighs its disadvantage of unfamiliarity, Wienbroer et al. recommend, "When you do use a technical term for a general audience, be sure to define or explain it" when first mentioning it.

Nominalizations often tend to weaken writing. Nominalizations are nouns derived from verbs, such as *collection* from *to collect*. They pose problems because too many nouns in a sentence as opposed to verbs make the sentence heavy and inert by focusing on the mere presence or existence of things rather than on what happens concerning them, as Lunsford and Connors illustrate in *The New St. Martin's Handbook:* "The *effect* of the *overuse* of *nouns* in *writing* is the *placing* of too much *stress* on the inadequate *number* of *verbs* and the resultant *prevention* of *movement* of the *thought*." The authors intentionally pile nominalizations into their sentence to produce the effect they describe. It would be quicker and easier to write and to read the alternative they provide: *"Overusing nouns places a big strain on the verbs and consequently slows down the prose."* Regarding nominalizations specifically, Lunsford and Connors add,

> Although nominalization can help make prose clearer and more concise—for example, using *abolition* instead of *the process of abolishing*—it can also produce the opposite effect, making a sentence unnecessarily wordy and hard to read.... Too often, writers use nominalizations not to make a complex process easier to talk about but to make an idea sound more complex and abstract than it really is.

This attempt to fancify writing usually backfires: it confuses less sophisticated readers and to more sophisticated readers appears like emperor's new clothes failing to hide rather bare content. Frequent use of the passive voice also creates weak writing. In the passive voice, the main action of the sentence is done to the main noun; in the active voice, by contrast, the main noun of the sentence does the main action. William Strunk and E. B. White in *The Elements of Style* provide two sentences stating the same idea to contrast the active and the passive voices:

ACTIVE VOICE: "I shall always remember my first visit to Boston."
PASSIVE VOICE: "My first visit to Boston will always be remembered by me."

Like nominalizations, the passive voice weakens writing by making it wordier and less action-oriented—we see the state of being remembered instead of the deed of remembering. The passive voice changes the natural order of thought, making the sentence convoluted and indirect. My Advanced Composition instructor in college taught me one case in which to prefer the passive voice, however: when the object of an action is more important than its subject. In the sentence "John F. Kennedy was assassinated by Lee Harvey Oswald," the man who was assassinated is placed first because he is more historically significant than the assassin and thereby catches our interest immediately; Lee Harvey Oswald is famous only for killing President Kennedy, but President Kennedy is famous for many things besides being killed.

Your writing will lose appeal while losing gravity if you do not choose your words with precision. A classic instance of this effect occurred during the 2004 presidential campaign when, in the midst of much conversation in Washington about "regime change" in Iraq, John Kerry said that it was time for "regime change" in the United States. His remark touched off a firestorm in the press; "regime" does not simply mean administration or leadership, but rather a type or system of government. "Regime change" in the United States would mean deposing the president, dissolving Congress, tearing up the Constitution, and rebuilding the government from scratch. Not only did Kerry's gaffe distract his audience from his real message, but it also showed he used the English language as incompetently as his notoriously inarticulate opponent.

Many cases of imprecision arise not from denotation (a word's definition) but from connotation, a word's emotional charge. My high school English teacher would point out that no one ever says, "The stench of her perfume delighted me" or "The aroma of the garbage nauseated me." Both *stench* and *aroma* are synonyms for *smell*, but we all know, almost by second nature, that the former is a negative term and the latter is a positive term. Sometimes this second nature fails us. When I tutored at the University of Maryland Writing Center as an undergraduate, a student wrote in her graduate school application essay, referring to an incident in her volunteer work, "I could comprehend their sorrow." I told her to replace *comprehend* with *understand*. Coming from Latin, "comprehend" has a more cerebral, intellectual connotation. "Understand," an Anglo-Saxon word, feels more visceral—it pertains more to the kind of emotional knowledge she was writing about.

Generally vague or abstract writing defeats the very purpose of communication: it prevents the audience from knowing just what the heck you're writing about. Professional and especially official writing is highly prone to vagueness and abstraction, and its writers often commit these flaws intentionally. Sentences without subjects constitute perhaps the most common kind of vague writing; Strunk and White note the weakness of phrases like "it is" or "there is" at the beginning of sentences, which render their subjects indefinite. Lunsford and Connors take this criticism further, showing that such phrases can serve a dissembling purpose: "A more subtle problem with these openings ... is that they may be used to avoid taking responsibility for a statement. Look at the following two sentences:

It is necessary to raise student fees.
The university must raise student fees.

The first sentence avoids responsibility by failing to tell us *who says* it is necessary." It shields the university from blame by hiding it from view, posing the issue of raising fees as if it were a force of nature.

Euphemisms provide another common device for intentional vagueness. *The New St. Martin's Handbook* defines euphemisms as "terms designed to make an unpleasant idea more attractive or acceptable"—such as *lady of the evening* for *prostitute*. Lunsford and Connors caution, "Use euphemisms with great care. Although they can appeal to readers by showing that the writer is considering their feelings, they can also sound pompous or suggest a wishy-washy, timid, or evasive attitude." They can also suggest that the writer's consideration of the audience's feelings is superficial: "*Your position is being eliminated* seeks to soften the blow of being fired or laid off." Lots of luck. Lunsford and Connors add, "Other euphemisms include *pass on* for *die* and *sanitation engineer* for *garbage collector*." Euphemisms of this last type are a sure sign of a style inspired by an inflated ego. A fellow member of my hometown writers' group constantly called himself a retired "elementary educator"; he even objected when I referred to him as a "teacher," as though that admirable title insulted him. Also beware of using common euphemisms outside of situations they are normally used in. When a telemarketer once asked for my aunt a minute after she had left the house, my father informed the caller, "She's no longer with us." That made it sound as if she had died.

Lunsford and Connors refer to the systematic, large-scale use of euphemisms to sanitize the disagreeable as "doublespeak." "The name given by George Orwell to the language of Big Brother in his novel *1984*, doublespeak is the use of language to hide or distort the truth," they explain. As the word implies, doublespeak usually tries to describe what it refers to as the opposite of what it actually is. Lunsford and Connors continue, "During the massive layoffs and cutbacks in the corporate and business worlds in recent years, companies continued to speak of firings and layoffs as *work reengineering, employee repositioning, proactive downsizing,* and *special reprogramming.* The public ... recognized this use of doublespeak." Call them what you will, it would take a profoundly stupid person to believe that these layoffs were anything other than de-positioning or de-programming. Moreover, "proactive downsizing," as opposed to "reactive," can only mean that this downsizing did not result from any external stimulus—company executives simply took people's employment away to line their own and their investors' pockets with more profits. Michael Stephens, the professor of my memoir workshop in graduate school at Emerson College, once declared, "Writing is the worst place in the world to hide."

The primary characteristics of good style, then, are the opposites of those of bad style: strength, precision, and specificity or concreteness. Strength has much to do with the ease with which the writer commands the language; directness, simplicity, and naturalness contribute tremendously to a piece of writing's strength. Simplicity in style does not require avoiding complex ideas—rather, your expression of them should be no more complicated in word choice, grammar, and structure than necessary. Since it holds that good writing resembles good speech, *Rules of Thumb for Business Writers* suggests that writers read their own work aloud as they write to train themselves in these qualities: "In time, your sentences will gain rhythm and force." *The New St. Martin's Handbook* suggests using figurative language—such as simile, metaphor, personification, hyperbole (exaggeration), metonymy (something associated with something else symbolizing it, *à la* "The pen is mightier than the sword") and synecdoche (a part of something representing the whole)—to strengthen style. In professional writing, one would want to use figurative language sparingly to prevent one's writing from sounding too extravagant or showy, but in small doses figurative language can succinctly convey complex or unusual ideas that might be difficult, lengthy, or tedious to explain in ordinary fashion.

To ensure strong style, base your writing on verbs. Our attention is naturally drawn to the dynamic, not the static; show your audience the action in what you write about. If there doesn't seem to be any action, put it in. Remember that grammatically, inanimate and insubstantial things can perform actions, in the manner of "The report provided several interpretations of the problem" or "The data demonstrated a dislike of company products." If keeping the verb in its true verb form proves too difficult or awkward, use a gerund instead of a nominalization. "Criticizing the manager could jeopardize my good standing," because it uses a participle form that can also be used as a verb, sounds stronger than "Criticism of the manager could jeopardize my good standing." Habitually using the active voice also goes a long way toward strengthening writing, as mentioned previously. "The active voice is usually more direct and vigorous than the passive," say Strunk and White. Like verb-based writing, it keeps our focus on the action of the sentence by showing it as it happens.

Precision in writing helps your audience understand your subject exactly as you want them to. Choosing a more precise word like *endorse* over its more general synonym, *support*, lets the audience in on a shade of significance that otherwise would be lost, that of lending the weight of one's reputation to the person or cause one favors. Precision renders writing fuller, more complete.

Proper use of connotation plays a major part in writing's precision; through connotation, writers can slant their writing to convey how they feel about their subject or to appeal to their audience's feelings about it. Lunsford and Connors observe, "What one reporter might call *a massive demonstration*, for example, another might call *a noisy protest*, and yet another, *an angry march*." Certainly, you should use words with positive connotations when writing about something you support and words with negative connotations when writing about something you oppose. Persuasive writing tends to employ connotation more than purely expository writing, but connotation can still be useful when interpreting information you present or even in presenting information that you or your audience feels or should feel positively or negatively about.

Writers have a few tools to help them use connotation properly. The best way is to use a thesaurus. Not only does a thesaurus provide a multitude of synonyms ranging the emotional gamut, but the best, like the *American Heritage Thesaurus*, provide blurbs on some of the more complicated entries explaining the shades of meaning among them. Dictionaries are another tool: some definitions will actually give the emotional value of the word, and the word origins given in larger reference dictionaries can offer clues about how the word registers emotionally. If, for some reason, neither the thesaurus nor the dictionary works in a particular situation, listen to your gut—or ask someone else what his or her gut feeling is when they hear the word you're considering.

I can, nonetheless, give you a general hint here. I keep mentioning that Latinate words sound loftier than Anglo-Saxon words. That's not merely due to the emphasis put on the ancient classics by the educational systems of yore; it's about politics. English, in a way, is a hybrid language. In the early Middle Ages, English vocabulary was exclusively Anglo-Saxon, Germanic. But when William the Conqueror took over England and Normans became the ruling class, they added a French stratum to the language's vocabulary. Soon, words derived from French—or from Latin by way of French—gained a polished, refined connotation because they were associated with how the nobility spoke; conversely, words derived from Anglo-Saxon, because they were associated with how the peasantry spoke, gained a coarse, crude connotation.

The great scholar of mythology Joseph Campbell gave a perfect example of this fact in one of his lectures: he noted that when a pig roots in dirt for its food and wallows in mud it's called *swine* (German: *schwein*), but when it's served in neat little cutlets on a platter, maybe with some garnish, it's *pork* (French: *porc*). At the time of the first Persian Gulf War, New York *Times* columnist William Safire explained why many people charged Saddam Hussein with "naked aggression" but nobody said he had committed "nude aggression." *Naked*, as an Anglo-

Saxon word (German: *nackt*), carries a crass connotation fitting Saddam's viciousness and brazenness. *Nude*, coming from French (*nu*—"bare") would have been too refined for the context. To corroborate Safire's explanation, let me say that in the campus art library where I worked all through college, we had quite a number of books with the phrase "nude photographs" in the title, but not once in four years did I see the words "naked photographs" grace a volume's spine.

Specific and concrete language forms a cornerstone of good style. Human beings learn best through experience; to make your readers understand what you're writing about, make them experience it through your writing. Strunk and White insist that "even when dealing with general principles, the writer must furnish particular instances of their application." Lunsford and Connors explain, "Because passages that contain mostly general terms or abstractions demand that readers supply most of the specific examples or concrete details with their imaginations, such writing is often hard to read." Vague or abstract writing demands that the reader do too much work to understand it. Specific, concrete writing is full-service writing. Failure to use specific and concrete writing begs the question "How?" from the reader—and often makes the reader suspect that you're holding something back, that you're afraid of stating what you want to state in full detail. Arthur H. Bell, in *NTC's Business Writer's Handbook*, says, "If the writer writes 'Frank is unreliable' (abstract) when he or she meant to communicate 'Frank comes to work late' (concrete), an abstract word has been misused." The misuse consists of its withholding the specific information of tardiness. More properly, *unreliable* would serve as a general complaint under which several specific complaints—not only untimeliness, but also maybe unproductivity and insubordination—would be elaborated.

Nonetheless, specificity and concreteness are not to be worshipped in and of themselves. Lunsford and Connors caution, "But writing that is full of specifics can also be tedious and hard to follow if the main point is not made clearly or is lost amid a flood of details. Strong writing must usually provide readers both with a general idea or overall picture and with specific examples or concrete details to fill in that picture." Facts and details should be used to illustrate topics and prove claims within a broader theme or argument. In most types of expository writing, the writer should subordinate them to the ideas that inform them or are derived from them. *The Elements of Style* reminds us, "It is not that every detail is given ... but that all the significant details are given."

These three building blocks of good style—strength, precision, and specificity or concreteness—unite to form one overarching edifice: clarity. George Orwell, cited earlier regarding doublespeak, once wrote, "Good prose is like a windowpane." In professional writing, nothing should come between the reader and the information communicated, neither the writer's ineptitude at written English nor his or her literary delusions of grandeur. If the way you write takes your audience's attention away your writing's content, your writing has failed. Together, strength, precision, and specificity or concreteness will keep you and your reader on the same page—literally and figuratively.

SENTENCE STRUCTURE

The word *text* comes from the same root as *textile*. A written work is a fabric woven from many individual threads—sentences. In a piece of writing, sentences should work together to form a clear overall design, but they can't if their threads are tangled or wander outside their place in the pattern. Hence the importance of good sentence structure, or syntax.

When you need to play it safe, stick to the simple sentence, which consists of a single independent clause. *The New St. Martin's Handbook* defines a clause as "a group of words containing a subject and a predicate," and continues, "Independent clauses ... can stand alone as complete sentences ..." Simple sentences can be as, well, simple and as brief as "She sang." The pronoun "she" serves as the subject, while the verb "sang" provides the grammatical minimum for a predicate.

Make the simple sentence your model as you write. "Short sentences are the meat and bones of good writing," declare Diana Roberts Wienbroer et al. in *Rules of Thumb For Business Writers*. They recommend, "Intersperse short sentences throughout your writing for clarity and strength.

- They can simplify an idea....
- They can add rhythm....
- They can be blunt and forceful."

In *The Elements of Style*, William Strunk and E. B. White argue, "Vigorous writing is concise. A sentence should contain no unnecessary words ... for the same reason that a drawing should have no unnecessary lines and a machine no unnecessary parts." The more elaborate or complex the machine, the more things can go wrong or the more difficult it may be to operate. The same holds true for writing: the more structurally involved the sentence, the greater the chance of error in syntax, grammar, or style by the writer or of confusion on the part of the reader. Simple sentences transmit information to the reader straightforwardly, with a minimum of internal distraction or interference.

In fact, most bad sentences fail because they stray too far from this mold—the writer bites off more than he or she can chew. British writer Kingsley Amis, in his book *The King's English*, recalls from his journalistic days a syntactical error over-enthusiastic fellow reporters fell prone to that he names the "gorged snake" sentence. Trying to pack as much information into one sentence as possible, they loaded it with clause after clause, phrase after phrase, until it stretched down the page for many lines, eventually too weighed down by its own mass to move the article forward. Strunk and White maintain, "When you become hopelessly mired in a sentence, it is best to start fresh; do not try to fight your way through against the terrible odds of syntax. Usually what is wrong is that the construction has become too involved at some point; the sentence needs to be broken apart and replaced by two or more shorter sentences."

Fortunately, all simple sentences don't have to look or sound alike. Most have more to them than only a noun and a verb; Wienbroer et al. observe, "Usually, a completer (a complement [the rest of the predicate besides the verb], direct object, or modifier) is added." Thus, our original simple sentence, "She sang," can be turned into

She sang while hearing us boo her.

or

　　　She sang *La Traviata.*

and remain a simple sentence.

　　　Wienbroer et al. also provide an easy way to vary the structure of simple sentences: begin some with an introductory phrase ending in a comma. As examples, they give the following:

　　　"However, the entertainment expenses have been disallowed.
　　　For example, we only use organic produce.
　　　In the packet labeled 'Open First,' you'll find the necessary tools."

Often, these introductory phrases contain what Angela Lunsford and Robert Connors, in *The New St. Martin's Handbook*, call conjunctive adverbs. "Conjunctive adverbs modify an entire clause and express the connection in meaning between that clause and the preceding clause (or sentence). Examples of conjunctive adverbs include *however, furthermore, therefore,* and *likewise*," they explain. The first of Wienbroer et al.'s example sentences above begins with a conjunctive adverb. Given that they relate their own sentence to the sentence before, introductory phrases with conjunctive adverbs work especially well in transitional sentences. Prepositional or participial phrases can also introduce a simple sentence, as in "To get there, turn left" or "Grasping firmly, she pulled the door's handle." Using this technique selectively can prevent monotony by reversing the sentence's normal order; ordinarily we would say "Turn left to get there" and "She pulled the door's handle, grasping firmly." Such occasional reversal keeps us on our toes, like syncopation in music.

　　　Varying the order of sentences can be important not only for syntax but for meaning. "The position of the words in a sentence is the principal means of showing their relationship," *The Elements of Style* teaches. To demonstrate, it renders a sample sentence written two different ways. The first sentence reads, "You can call your mother in London and tell her all about George's taking you out to dinner for just two dollars." Most readers would be immediately either amazed or skeptical to hear of a restaurant serving a full meal for such a low price. Then the second sentence clarifies the situation: "For just two dollars you can call your mother in London and tell her all about George's taking you out to dinner." After the first sentence's two main verbs, *call* and *tell*, the gerund *taking* ensues; if we leave the prepositional phrase "for just two dollars" in its usual place at the end of the sentence, we instinctively assume it modifies the closest verb (sort of), *taking*. To ensure that the reader understands what "for just two dollars" refers to, we need to move it to the start of the sentence where nothing else it could possibly modify intervenes between it and *call*. (Alternatively, we could write, "You can call your mother in London for just two dollars ...") Moreover, placing "for just two dollars" at the beginning calls the reader's attention to the affordability of the long distance service—evidently this writer's point—because it strikes him or her immediately.

　　　The primacy of the simple sentence does not forbid us to go beyond it at times; life itself seldom permits us to rely on the simple sentence alone. You will often write about complex ideas and facts that require more elaborate sentence structure to adequately and accurately express them and the relationships among them. Different kinds of sentence structure can be used for different purposes. "A children's story, for instance, may call for mostly short sentences whereas an article on nuclear disarmament in the *Atlantic* may call for considerably longer ones," Lunsford and Connors tell us. Long sentences have a part to play in writing just as 300-pound linemen have a part to play in football. But those linemen only succeed if they have 300 pounds of muscle, not fat. Feel free to write long sentences when necessary as long as you ensure that every word in the sentence does work and isn't just flab. And make them the exception, not the rule.

The New St. Martin's Handbook reviews other types of sentence structure. The first, the compound sentence, "consists of two or more independent clauses and no dependent clause." Essentially, the compound sentence fuses what could be two separate sentences into one. Lunsford and Connors continue, "The clauses may be joined by a comma and a coordinating conjunction"—like *and*, *but*, or *or*, which relate the two clauses to each other—"or by a semicolon." We can turn one of our simple sentences from the previous section into compound sentences like so:

> We booed her; undaunted, she sang *La Traviata.*
> We booed her, but she sang *La Traviata* undaunted.

As with any literary device, the compound sentence should not be used arbitrarily. For the sentence to work, the subjects of its two independent clauses should be related; they must be distinct grammatically, but they should be two facets of a common theme. In our sample sentences above, the two independent clauses state two events occurring simultaneously and in reaction to each other.

The complex sentence employs a different structure. "A complex sentence consists of one independent clause and at least one dependent clause," *The New St. Martin's Handbook* says. By the way, dependent clauses "cannot stand alone as complete sentences," in the words of the *Handbook*, "... for they begin with a subordinating word—a subordinating conjunction or a relative pronoun—that connects them to an independent clause.

> *Because the window is open,* the room feels cool."

The *Handbook* also notes that dependent clauses often serve as adjectives or adverbs modifying the independent clause and often begin with subordinating conjunctions, which

> introduce adverb clauses and signal the relationship between the adverb clause and another clause, usually an independent clause. For instance, in the following sentence the subordinating conjunction *while* signals a time relationship, letting us know that the two events in the sentence happened simultaneously:

> > Sweat ran down my face *while* I frantically searched for my child.
> > *Unless* sales improve dramatically, the company will soon be bankrupt.
> > My grandmother began traveling *after* she sold her house.

Usually, the complex sentence is used when the idea in the dependent clause is a condition or contingency of the idea in the independent clause. The conjunction *while* tells us not only that sweat ran down the speaker's face at the same time he or she frantically searched for his or her child, but also—by implication—that this happened because of the search; likewise, in the third sentence, the dependent clause gives the time frame and reason for the action related in the independent clause. The second sentence's dependent clause presents the condition for avoiding bankruptcy. Our example might look like this as a complex sentence:

As soon as we left, she stopped singing.

Then there is the compound-complex sentence. You guessed it: a combination of the two former kinds. "A compound-complex sentence consists of two or more independent clauses and at least one dependent clause," say Lunsford and Connors. Thus, it combines two grammatically complete sentences, one of which must be a complex sentence. The other can be simple,

She sang, but as soon as we left, she stopped singing.

compound,

We booed her, but she sang *La Traviata* undaunted; as soon as we left, she stopped singing.

or even complex as well.

She sang while we booed her; as soon as we left, she stopped singing.

The compound-complex sentence combines the compound sentence and the complex sentence logically as well as structurally. The independent clauses should express interrelated ideas as in the compound sentence, and at least one dependent clause should include a condition or contingency as in the complex sentence. The compound-complex sentence is the most elaborate sentence form, but also the most supple: with a broad palette of punctuation, one can probably write several compound-complex sentences without exactly duplicating any particular format for them.

Other ways to address sentence structure exist if we expand its scope beyond grammatical form. *The New St. Martin's Handbook* also classifies sentences functionally, as declarative (statements), imperative (commands), exclamatory, or interrogative (questions). Declarative sentences form the bedrock of your prose. Imperative sentences in professional writing will mostly be limited to procedure instructions; exclamations, as noted in the punctuation chapter, bespeak an unprofessional boisterousness or flamboyance. Questions, however, can come in handy at times: they're a good way to formulate a problem, and also engage the reader by challenging him or her to arrive at your answer while reading along. *Rules of Thumb For Business Writers* propounds the stylistic advantage of using questions: "Replace implied questions with direct ones and your writing will sound more like a real conversation....

Indirect: Please determine whether we are responsible for undelivered back orders.
Direct: Are we responsible for undelivered back orders? Please let us know."

It also indicates that in cases like this where the question actually asks the reader for information, writing the question as such impresses the need for information more boldly upon the reader.

Don't fill your writing with questions, though. A piece of writing containing questions for every major point will feel contrived: they will come across as a failed attempt to hide an inability to transition between ideas, state problems, or express paradoxes in compelling declarative sentences. Furthermore, while the Socratic method of teaching by asking questions rather than answering them (or at least greatly postponing the answers) may work wonders in the classroom, it will tend to annoy professionals pressed for time by delaying your and their arrival at the solution, their real interest.

Additionally, *The New St. Martin's Handbook* classifies sentences—mainly long ones—rhetorically, into two kinds. "Cumulative sentences, which begin with an independent clause and then add details and phrases and other clauses, are far more common than periodic sentences," it tells us. "They are useful when you want to provide both immediate understanding of the main idea and a great deal of supporting detail." Perhaps the most famous cumulative sentence in English is the climax of the Declaration of Independence: "We hold these truths to be self-evident, that all men are created equal, that they are endowed by their Creator with certain unalienable Rights, that among these are Life, Liberty, and the pursuit of Happiness." The cumulative sentence submits a general principle and breaks it down into specific examples and constituent parts, extracting its corollaries. Use a cumulative sentence to express ideas involving deductive reasoning, arriving at particular ideas through general ones.

"Periodic sentences," Lunsford and Connors's other rhetorical classification, "postpone the main idea (usually in an independent clause) until the very end of a sentence. Effectively written periodic sentences are especially useful for creating tension or building toward a climactic or surprise ending." The next-to-last paragraph of Henry David Thoreau's *Walden* offers a great example of the periodic sentence:

> Who knows what beautiful and winged life, whose egg has been buried for ages under many concentric layers of woodenness in the dead dry life of society, deposited at first in the alburnum of the green and living tree, which has gradually been converted into the semblance of its well-seasoned tomb,—heard perchance gnawing out now for years by the astonished family of man, as they sat round the festive board,—may unexpectedly come forth from amidst society's most trivial and handselled furniture, to enjoy its perfect summer life at last!

The periodic sentence proceeds like a legal argument, accumulating evidence that leads up to an inevitable conclusion—or, in the case of the surprise ending referred to by Lunsford and Connors, the opposite of a seemingly inevitable conclusion. It works best with ideas involving inductive reasoning, which derives general ideas from particulars.

Neither the cumulative sentence nor the periodic sentence should be mistaken for the run-on sentence or Amis's "gorged snake" sentence. Rhetorical sentences contain one main thought and several supporting thoughts building up to or extending out from them, and maintain thematic integrity; run-on sentences collect and mix several loosely related or unrelated thoughts in a manner that gives none of them precedence over the others, and do not effectively unite their thoughts to one another. You should always be able to identify a single idea as the main topic of your sentence.

I know all this sounds easier said than done. I can tell you about the various types of sentences and the rationale for using each type, but only you can determine for yourself at the time of writing when to use each one. We writers simply cannot get around that. *Rules of Thumb For Business Writers* advises, "Write important sentences several ways until you find the best phrasing." Writing is experimental, experiential; often you don't know what you need until you realize you can't use what you have.

PARAGRAPH STRUCTURE

A piece of writing resembles a ladder its reader must climb. Its introduction acts as its base, where the reader begins the ascent; its top is the conclusion, the reader's destination after moving through its body. That body consists of rungs that, one by one, bring the reader closer to the piece of writing's conclusion and allows him or her to arrive there on solid footing. Those rungs are paragraphs. In *The Elements of Style*, William Strunk and E. B. White instruct, "Make the paragraph the unit of composition." Therefore, structuring your paragraphs well contributes immensely to effective writing.

Let's start at the beginning, with the paragraph's introductory sentence—usually a topic sentence, stating a new idea in the development of your thesis or subject. The break in text created by a new paragraph's indentation announces this change. Angela Lunsford and Robert Connors elaborate in *The New St. Martin's Handbook*: "Remember that a new paragraph often signals a pause in thought. Just as timing can make a crucial difference in telling a joke, so the pause signaled by a paragraph can lead readers to anticipate what is to follow ..." If what follows does not present a new idea, readers are apt to be disappointed or confused.

The new idea expressed in the topic sentence should encapsulate the content of the ensuing paragraph. "Each paragraph should make one point, and every sentence in it should relate to that one point," declare Diana Roberts Wienbroer et al. in *Rules of Thumb For Business Writers*. The topic sentence provides the thematic baseline around which all other sentences in the paragraph must revolve.

Wienbroer et al. give a simple reason for placing the paragraph's declaration of intent at its start: most readers in a professional setting are pressed for time and want information presented to them as quickly and smoothly as possible. Beginning a paragraph with its topic tells the reader what to expect ahead, rather than making the reader guess at where your writing is going as he or she reads along. On the other hand, Lunsford and Connors argue rightly when they say, "When specific details add up to a generalization, putting the topic sentence at the end of the paragraph makes sense." This strategy suits works relying on inductive reasoning, moving from particular points toward a larger common idea; it can also lend variety to the structural pattern of your paragraphs. With the exception of legal writing or laboratory or survey reports, however, few occasions for inductive logic arise in professional writing.

Sometimes, instead of or in addition to staking out new territory for a composition, the first sentence of a paragraph connects the preceding paragraph to this new idea. "Link your paragraphs together with transitions—taking words or ideas from one paragraph and using them at the beginning of the next," suggests *Rules of Thumb For Business Writers*. Transition sentences at the beginning of a paragraph work best when the main idea of its paragraph grows out of, is a corollary of, or is an antithesis to that of the preceding paragraph. For example, the first sentence of this paragraph introduces the theme of the transition sentence by contrasting it with the preceding paragraphs' theme of making a break from the rest of the text.

The body of a paragraph works to support its topic statement. As you flesh out a paragraph, "ask yourself ... how each sentence develops the paragraph topic," say Lunsford and Connors. Because, they assert, a paragraph "focuses on one main idea (unity); its parts are clearly related (coherence); and its main idea is supported with specifics (development)." Demonstrate explicitly and thoroughly how your details support your topic, especially where your interpretation of how they do is novel or counterintuitive. Drive the point home. Don't leave any gaps in your argument, assuming that your reader will be clever enough to carry your line of reasoning over them; readers don't expect to do your work for you, and your carefully built argument may appear to the reader like a house of cards.

"Within a paragraph, make sure that your sentences follow a logical sequence," Wienbroer et al. insist. "Each one should build upon the previous one and lead to the next." They recommend, "If you have trouble with paragraph organization, you can usually rely on this basic paragraph pattern:

> A main point stated in one sentence
> An explanation of any general words in your main point
> An example or details that support your point
> The reason each example or detail supports your point
> A sentence to sum up"

You may also find it helpful to preface some supports, if they are different in kind, with an explanation of this difference to help the reader switch mental gears between them, or with transitions if they are similar in kind. "In acting as signposts, transitions such as *after all, for example, indeed, so,* and *thus* help readers follow the progression of one idea to the next within a paragraph," says *The New St. Martin's Handbook*. "*Finally* indicates that a last point is at hand; *likewise*, that a similar point is about to be made, and so on." Other common transitions include

Also	In addition	Additionally	Furthermore
Moreover	Similarly	By comparison	By contrast
However	Nonetheless	Still	Therefore
In spite of	Despite	First (Second, etc.)	To begin
Lastly	To conclude	In conclusion	Next

"It is important to note," the *Handbook* cautions, "that transitions can only clarify connections between thoughts; they cannot create connections." As with linking supports to your paragraph's main idea, make the relationships between supports as explicit as possible if someone less familiar with your topic would not find them readily apparent. Transitions between similar supports, and introductions before supports of differing types, tell the reader that your argument in that paragraph is solid and cohesive because of its uniformity or in spite of its variety—they suggest that your supports are more than a random collection of incidences, that they form a trend of evidence of your topic statement's truth. Merely planting a transition word into a paragraph without explaining the connection could seem to your readers like hastily brushing over an incongruity in your argument and may raise doubts in their minds about your argument's validity.

Parallel structure provides another strategy for giving unity to a paragraph; "[e]xpress coordinate ideas in similar form," Strunk and White recommend. They illustrate this principle with the Sermon on the Mount, in which each sentence has two clauses that start the same way: "Blessed are the [blank]; they shall [blank]." This device conveys the similarity between or among points more dramatically, embodying it through grammar and syntax.

The importance of unity in your paragraph necessitates avoiding digressions. Some of your supports—especially more complex , specialized, or arcane ones—may require more elaboration or explanation than usual, or may require you to define terms or supply background information. That's fine. Just keep such material to the minimum necessary to elucidate your topic; don't let it create a tangent that leads you away from your paragraph's line of thought. Enclosing digressions in parentheses or pairs of dashes can assist you in limiting their length.

That leaves us with the concluding sentence. A concluding sentence should recap the paragraph's main point and summarize its content. "Sometimes you will want to state a topic sentence at the beginning of a paragraph and then refer to it in a slightly different form at the end," Lunsford and Connors suggest. "Such an echo of the topic sentence adds emphasis, pointing up the importance you attach to the idea." Make sure this reiteration does differ in form, and maybe more than slightly. If you can't rephrase the main idea from a different angle, you'd be better off leaving the concluding sentence out than parroting to the reader what he or she has already read.

Best of all, the angle from which you rephrase your paragraph's main idea should be the body of the paragraph: state what about the main idea you have learned from your paragraph's material, what the reader can take away from the paragraph that he or she didn't know at its beginning. In addition, if the topic of the next paragraph derives from or relates to something in the current paragraph, your concluding sentence can lead into or set up the transition to or presentation of that idea in the following paragraph's introductory sentence.

How long should a paragraph be? At the risk of sounding smart-alecky, it should be long enough to prove your main idea. As mentioned earlier, some items in a paragraph may require more extensive treatment than others; so may some paragraphs and their topics. "Paragraphs should be as long as they need to be to make one point," Wienbroer et al. assert—no longer, no shorter.

Wienbroer et al. offer ways of dealing with underdeveloped or overdeveloped paragraphs: "If you have a string of paragraphs which consist of one or two sentences, you may need to combine, develop, or omit some of your paragraphs.

COMBINE
- Join two paragraphs about the same point.
- Include examples in the same paragraph as the point they illustrate....

DEVELOP
- Explain any important general terms."

If neither combining nor expanding works for a stunted paragraph, they advise, "chances are that paragraph should be dropped. Sometimes you have to decide whether you really want to explain a particular point or whether it's not important." Prepare yourself to leave out an idea you like very much, even your favorite idea on your subject, if you can't make it hold its own weight. Prepare to give up what you want for the sake of what the writing wants. Writers refer to this as "killing your babies."

On the other side of the coin, "A paragraph that is more than ten sentences long usually should be divided. Find a natural point for division, such as:

- A subtopic

- A variation or contradiction
- The start of an example"

Frankly, I find the limit of ten sentences arbitrary; don't base your decision on a hard-and-fast number, but on whether the paragraph is longer than you would want to read yourself.

After all, spatial considerations, as well as the sufficiency of its argument, contribute to the proper length of a paragraph. "Paragraphs give readers a visual landing, a place to pause," explains *Rules of Thumb For Business Writers*; a paragraph's length relates to your reader's attention span, and an inordinately long paragraph will likely ask the reader to stretch his or her attention span beyond its limit. Thus, "the trend in modern business writing is to avoid long paragraphs." *The Elements of Style* concurs: "Enormous blocks of print look formidable to readers, who are often reluctant to tackle them. Therefore, breaking long paragraphs in two, even if it is not necessary to do so for sense, meaning, or logical development, is often a visual help."

But sometimes you won't be able to find a good place to divide a long paragraph; sometimes a long paragraph does need everything in it that makes it long. At the same time, a short paragraph between two longer ones can be refreshing for readers, giving them time to catch their breath. Varying paragraph length can be as important in making your writing lively as varying sentence length. You'll just have to weigh the demands of your argument, the look of your writing on the page, and your audience's expectations against one another in each writing situation.

If a work of writing is like a ladder, a paragraph is too: its first and last sentences are the two ends, and each sentence of its body forms a rung. A paragraph is a composition in miniature, a microcosm of the argument it is a part of. These smaller arguments, each about a different aspect of your subject or thesis, combine to make up your overall argument—only if they all function soundly will your audience be interested, informed, and influenced.

OVERALL WRITING STRUCTURE

It's not always easy to structure professional writing. As Diana Roberts Wienbroer et al. observe in *Rules of Thumb For Business Writers*, "Writing in the business world is not like the writing that succeeds with teachers. In school, you write to demonstrate what you have learned." On the job, however, we seldom write primarily to display our abilities, but rather to produce certain results: your company taking on a new project, promoting an employee, encouraging investment. Accordingly, the standard five-paragraph high school essay—designed as a template for students to neatly organize and discuss the ideas treated in class—may not suffice when analyzing real-world actions and their consequences.

Nonetheless, that model of introduction, three paragraphs of argument, and conclusion provides valuable training for more complex kinds of writing. Michael Degen, a writing teacher, writes in *Creating Expository Argument* that introduction, body, and conclusion comprise the fundamental parts of nonfiction writing; Angela Lunsford and Robert Connors note in *The New St. Martin's Handbook*, and Aristotle demonstrates in his *Rhetoric*, that this pattern has been followed since antiquity. The academic five-paragraph essay may reduce this pattern to its simplest and least practical form, but it does develop the habit of structuring and supporting an argument, which will be useful once one moves on to writing requiring a more elaborate form— like professional writing.

Many ways exist for the business writer to structure his or her work. The best one for a particular instance will depend on the nature of the material and, especially, the approach one wants to take to it.

Intended as a stylistic rulebook for successful legal arguments, Aristotle's *Rhetoric* is the classic guide to expository writing. It describes the purpose of a piece of writing's introduction as "to make clear what is the end or purpose ... wherefore it should not be employed, if the subject is quite clear ..." Smaller works or works within a series may get by without one, in the former case because the topics dealt with aren't complex enough (or treated complexly enough) to require orienting the reader, and in the latter case because the reader already knows the piece's main themes from prior pieces in the series. A few years ago, I wrote summaries of several focus groups and interviews about a client's potential future product; since all the summaries were presented together and each was only a page or two long, I omitted introductions for the summaries that didn't stand out as unique. Major writing projects usually require an introduction. Select your occasions for dispensing with the introduction wisely: although doing so offers the virtue of conciseness, Aristotle warns that the introduction's "absence makes the speech appear offhand."

The introduction also captures the reader's attention and concern, or ought to. "Hearers pay most attention to things that are important, that concern their own interests, that are astonishing, that are agreeable; wherefore one should put the idea into their heads that the speech deals with these subjects," Aristotle argues. Use the introduction to convince readers that your writing is relevant to them and worth their while. Don't rest content in the fact that duty compels your boss to read your report; *impel* him or her to read on by showing in your introduction the report's value to his or her work.

An introduction should be shaped like a funnel, starting from the broad and general and ending with the narrow and specific. I usually begin introductions with a topic sentence stating the issue that my composition concerns. In my Advanced Composition class in college, I wrote a proposal to the Washington Metropolitan Area Transit Authority for running another Metrobus route through the University of Maryland campus; the first sentence of my proposal related the fact that such a large state college attracts a lot of activity from and generates a lot of activity in its environs, and therefore availability of adequate transportation to and from campus is essential. A topic sentence provides the context for your argument, demonstrates that it comes out of a real need in the world and doesn't arise from a vacuum. If you can ground your writing early on in a significant issue, your readership will more likely believe that what you have to say is worth reading. A writer can achieve this, *The New St. Martin's Handbook* elaborates, with a topic sentence that "contains ... a strong lead, or hook, to attract readers' interest.... A writer can ... begin an introduction with a *vivid statement* of the problem that led to the thesis or with an *intriguing quotation*, an *anecdote*, a *question*, or a *strong opinion*."

After presenting your topic, narrow your focus toward your thesis by describing what aspects of your topic play a part in the specific situation your thesis addresses. I used this part of my bus proposal's introduction to note that many commuter students and university employees rely on public transportation to get to campus and home again and many dorm students use it to travel in the surrounding area—and that the single Metrobus route running through campus at the time could not possibly accommodate most of them. Further, "[t]he introduction may include a history of the situation and a clear statement of the problem to be solved," writes Arthur H. Bell in *NTC's Business Writer's Handbook*. Any other general "necessary background" to your topic, in Wienbroer et al.'s words, should be included here as well. You would also develop the relevance of your topic to your audience or challenge your audience's perception of it, per Aristotle's dicta, in this middle part of your introduction.

Your thesis statement—the declaration of exactly what you are arguing—should cap your introduction. Lunsford and Connors teach, "A successful working thesis has three characteristics:

1. It is potentially *interesting* to your intended audience.
2. It is as *specific* as possible.
3. It limits the topic enough to make it *manageable*."

The thesis of my bus proposal, that the transit authority should run another bus route through the University of Maryland campus, met these criteria. My intended audience was the transit authority's director of planning for Maryland. He had reason to find interest in my proposal: I offered insight into the attitudes of the silent majority of riders who don't take the time to call or write to the transit authority about issues affecting them; I suggested a way for the transit authority to enhance its presence in the area and compete as a viable alternative to private transportation; and, most importantly, I dangled the carrot of new fare revenue in front of him. I also delineated a specific route that I believed included the most common and necessary destinations of the university population not serviced by the existing route. Restricting my proposal to increasing service by a single route made it more manageable for me to complete and more manageable for the transit authority to commit to.

"In many cases, especially when the writer begins with a quotation or an anecdote, the introduction consists of two paragraphs," observe Lunsford and Connors, "the first providing the hook and the second, an explanation of its significance." Alternatively, the first paragraph may focus on the general topic and the second paragraph may pivot to the specifics regarding it that lead up to your thesis. A double-paragraph introduction works best for topics that require a lot of background information for their discussion; they break up what could be a drawn-out, imposing initial block of prose into bite-sized chunks.

Now that you have an introduction, how do you organize what you've introduced? Several methods of development fit business writing (and one particularly does not), some functioning particularly well with certain kinds of projects.

Classification is one of the most common methods of development in expository writing. In it, the writer argues the thesis by discussing different types, categories, or examples of the situation the thesis pertains to, breaking the key idea of the thesis into constituent parts. I won a college scholarship from the National Cooperative Bank for an essay arguing that cooperatives provide many benefits to their members, their consumers, and society as a whole. I used classification to organize the essay; each paragraph described a certain effect of cooperatives and explained why it constituted a benefit. I began by stating that cooperatives' democratic structure means members have control over the practices of the business that serves them. Thus, members keep the cooperative and its officers directly accountable to themselves: officers will be unlikely to pursue policies or procedures that members dislike knowing that the members could vote to discontinue them or to remove the officers. I mentioned that cooperatives, by providing an alternative to private enterprise, influence private businesses to be more accountable and responsive to the public in order to compete with cooperatives for goodwill. Last but not least, cooperatives offer the financial rewards of lower prices (thanks to fewer middlemen and not as much profit motive) for consumer co-ops and stronger bargaining power for producer co-ops, as well as the members' profit dividend for each business period. Because classification is a leading method of development, ask yourself these questions formulated by Bell when stuck on how to arrange your material: "How can your main idea be divided into parts? How can those parts, and subdivisions within those parts, be arranged and classified?"

Lunsford and Connors call the next most common method of development "association—how bits of information are related in terms of images, motifs, ... and so on." Put more simply, it organizes material through shared ideas and thematic links. It operates similarly to classification, but relies on looser connections; the various ideas that organize the material don't have to add up to one overarching concept. In those focus group summaries I referred to, I first wrote about the participants' familiarity with and use of similar products, then about their attitudes toward participating in a trial of the new product, and lastly about what might increase their likelihood to participate. I aligned the themes of each section into a continuum of their experience with that type of product—from actual to hypothetical, from spontaneous to controlled.

The definition of the key term in your thesis can also provide a way of organizing your writing by discussing and perhaps comparing "the different significations of a word," as Aristotle says, or by tracing the implications of a definition. To start up your engines on this method of development, *NTC's Business Writer's Handbook* suggests asking yourself, "How can your main idea be defined? What are key terms within that definition? What is an operational or functional definition of your main idea?" When I was a tutor at the University of Maryland Writing Center I worked with a music student on an ingenious essay claiming that most musical instruments fall into the category of percussion. He found a dictionary definition of *percussion* as "striking," then found a dictionary definition of *strike* as basically to make any kind of contact as a result of motion. Thus, he argued, brass and woodwind instruments are percussion because one presses or

61

taps the keys or stops, the guitar is percussion because the plectrum strikes the strings, and the violin and cello are "struck" by moving the bow over their strings; presumably, only a few oddballs like the kazoo, the concertina, and the theremin might defy this definition.

Business writers often present their material in decreasing order of importance, as cited by Bell. Familiar from the "inverted pyramid" model of newspaper articles, this method of development starts with a brief summary of the most essential information about the subject (who, what, where, when, why, how—as in the lead of a news story) and continues by elaborating on this information and adding less important information. The decreasing-order-of-importance technique is suited for busy readers who want what they need to know fast and up front. Such readers will, consequently, likely overlook that this method of development makes for very dry reading.

Its opposite, presenting information in increasing order of importance, doesn't see much action in professional writing. As described by Bell, "The increasing-order-of-importance method of development places the most important item last, but tells the reader or listener at the beginning of the message about that order of development.... [T]hey read on knowing that the report will climax with the most relevant or valuable material." Bell is right that increasing order of importance offers the audience a sense of suspense or build-up. Most audiences in the professional world, however, don't have the time or absence of distraction on the job to appreciate this benefit that they would when delving into their favorite mystery novel at home. Avoid this method of development: don't test your readers' patience.

As Lunsford and Connors comment, writers also often arrange their professional writing by chronology. Bell writes, "The divisions of time—past, present, future—can provide an organizational pattern helpful to both the business communicator and his or her audience." Most occasions for professional writing probably call for simple chronological development, beginning with the past and continuing to the present—and perhaps concluding with projections for the future. Sometimes, nonetheless, you may want to move backward from the present to the past, for instance if your writing aims to diagnose the causes of current conditions (you could still conclude with predictions of future results based on your findings). You may even begin with a scenario of the future and explain its origins in the present and past, or the past and then the present. Numerous types of business writing lend themselves to the chronological method of development: company annual reports, project progress reports, meeting minutes, employee recommendations and reviews, and more.

A corollary of the chronological method of development is narrative. Personal narrative can be useful in legal briefs and arguments, incident reports, secret shopper reports, some letters, and proposals or other persuasive writing where anecdotal support could enhance your argument. Non-personal narrative, though, takes an even more prominent place in professional writing. *NTC's Business Writer's Handbook* remarks that most annual reports have a narrative section discussing company developments in several areas; you can gain your readers' interest by making this section truly narrative. Things shouldn't just *happen* in your report, the company should *do* them—make your company its own story's protagonist, whom its shareholders can identify with as they encounter its accomplishments and struggles along with it in the narrative.

That said, narrative might not work in some writing situations—particularly those primarily data-driven. In a report of laboratory or survey findings, in fact, the desired feeling of anonymous objectivity and impartiality demands that those conducting the study stay in the writing's background, whereas narrative places its agent in the foreground. A remark-by-remark account of the focus groups in my summaries would have included a lot of extraneous junk and been painfully boring; I organized it thematically and selectively around responses to key questions asked by the moderator instead. Don't force yourself to tell a story where none exists.

Bell adds, "As a general rule, relatively formal and official business communications prefer third person narration for its objectivity." Your professional writing will probably call for discussing others' experiences rather than your own anyway. In types of writing like secret shopper reports, however, first-person narration is practically unavoidable.

Reports analyzing a nationwide company's performance customarily adopt the spatial method of development, segmenting their analysis by regions of the country: New England, the Mid-Atlantic, the Midwest, *et cetera*. Lunsford and Connors cite space as one of the ways "writers most often group information," and their example shows the perhaps obvious applicability of this method to projects focusing on facilities or physical plant: "A report on a college library's accessibility to students in wheelchairs, for example, might describe the spaces in the library that are most often used and then evaluate their accessibility to a student in a wheelchair—one room or space or area at a time." While "[m]ost business communications involving narration make use of the chronological pattern of development.... Narration can also follow spatial order, telling about circumstances far away to near at hand, or vice versa," affirms Bell. Spatial development combines directly with narration in secret shopper reports in which the shopper relates his or her progress through each department or section of the store.

Such an approach in turn illustrates why Lunsford and Connors comment, "In much of your writing, you will want to combine two or more organizational patterns." You can use one pattern to organize your writing into paragraphs or sections and another to discuss the material within each paragraph or section. Continuing the example of the secret shopper report, one could devote a paragraph to each section of the store, discussing in each paragraph what occurred from the time one entered that section to the time one left it. You can think of the two patterns as the x and y axes on which to "plot" your writing, or the warp and woof on which to weave it.

When translating your method of development into the actual body of your composition, don't leave any conceptual gaps in your writing. *The New St. Martin's Handbook* cautions writers to "ask yourself how each paragraph relates to or supports the thesis" and to ask themselves, "Can you identify clear links between paragraphs and ideas? Do any others need to be added? Have any important points been left out?" Demonstrate your thesis as thoroughly as possible within the length restrictions or expected scope of your piece of writing.

On a similar note, include any special information needed to understand your material and to follow your discussion if your audience may not possess it already. This information differs from the more basic historical or situational overview of your topic that you may put in your introduction; here, you would establish or clarify the dimensions of your specific problem or argument. Subjects with unique jargon that may need defining, or with technical or more precise meanings for general terms, are prime candidates for this kind of explanatory information. "A magazine article about poverty in the United States, for example, would have to define very carefully what level of income, assets, or other measure defines a person, family, or household as 'poor,'" explain Lunsford and Connors. The article would do this *after* presenting a brief overview of the subject of poverty in the United States and making the particular claim about it that it intends to prove—the reader wants as little as possible to intervene between raising your subject at the start of your introduction and arriving at the piece of writing's point, your thesis. Still, place such explanatory material at the beginning of the body to give your reader all the tools needed to dig into the ensuing meat of your writing.

Don't let your readers lose sight of your thesis or main idea over the course of your writing. *Rules of Thumb For Business Writers* advises, "Repetition of a major point is often necessary in a long document. At times, you may choose to repeat a point to give it added weight. When you do repeat a point, make sure that you use slightly different wording and that you place each repetition in a slightly different context." Specifically, repeat your main idea in the first sentence of a paragraph in terms of that paragraph's topic, or in the last sentence of a paragraph in terms of the conclusions you can draw from that paragraph's material.

One way to keep your writing cohesive and your audience aware of its progression and their place in it goes beyond its content or your treatment of it, which your audience may not have the leisure to benefit from immediately. Wienbroer et al. explain, "Readers in business often want only the point. In most cases, you must provide the rationale or the details, but those should be subordinated to a place where the busy reader can skim them. Headings, bulleted lists ... will allow the reader to see the difference between the point and the supporting information." Although incidental, strategically placing these and other typographical road signs in your writing can give your audience a taste of what follows and a welcome sense that they, and you, are staying on track.

"On some occasions, you may need to call your readers' attention very powerfully to a major transition between ideas," write Lunsford and Connors. "To do so, consider using an entire short paragraph to signal that transition ..." Transitioning between parts of your document with a short paragraph can add variety and counterpoint to the flow of your writing and give your readers a breather from longer, denser paragraphs. No less revered an authority than good old Aristotle regularly introduces new subjects, which he then spends several long paragraphs dividing and classifying, with short paragraphs.

You can also use dialogue to lighten the weight of a document laden with thick slabs of paragraphs. "Paragraphs of dialogue can add life to almost any sort of writing," Lunsford and Connors attest. "The traditional way to set up dialogue in written form is simple: start a new paragraph each time the speaker changes, no matter how short each bit of conversation is." Dialogue won't appear as much in professional writing as in fiction or even general nonfiction, but it does have its place there. It can record exchanges with store employees in secret shopper reports and relate parts of the discussion in a focus group summary. Actually, the quoted speech of a single person more commonly finds its way into professional writing than "dialogue" proper. Individual speech can be included within a paragraph of your own text—in quotation marks, of course—and can provide a less dramatic but effective change of voice, style, and tempo embedded within your paragraph.

Many writers, once they have said everything they intend to say, conclude by simply summarizing the body of their piece of writing. This is one of the most habitual mistakes in expository writing, and one of the oldest. Aristotle proclaims in the *Rhetoric* that "the conclusion must neither be drawn from too far back"—it should not reference particular details presented all the way in the beginning, which are no longer in the front of the reader's mind— "nor should it include all the steps of the argument. In the first case its length causes obscurity, in the second, it is simply a waste of words, because it states much that is obvious." The reader does not need to be told everything twice.

Rather, your conclusion should be designed like the inverse of your introduction: beginning with a statement narrowly applicable to your thesis or main point and progressing outward toward a broader relevance. *The New St. Martin's Handbook* states, "Often a conclusion will begin with a restatement of the thesis and end with more general statements that grow out of it: this pattern reverses the common general-to-specific pattern of the introduction." The initial statement can briefly summarize or encapsulate the gist of your argument, but should soon move past it. Your conclusion should work toward the lesson of the piece of writing, what the reader should take away from it—it should answer the reader's hypothetical question, "Now that I know this, so what?" "Discuss implications and questions that your report brings to mind," *Rules of Thumb For Business Writers* bids us. The *Handbook* recommends several devices for powerfully wrapping up a work of writing, "including a *provocative question*, a *quotation*, a *vivid image*, a *call for action*, a *warning*." A call for action or a warning are the most customary of these ways in business writing; using a vivid image leans more toward creative writing, but can have a place in the professional world, as I will demonstrate right now.

The structure of a typical piece of business writing resembles an elongated hourglass. At the top it opens wide to take in general issues and subjects from the outer world and funnels them into a narrower, more particular thesis; at its bottom it opens from that tightened scope into the world again by offering the practical significance of your discussion. The body of a piece of writing represents a passageway much longer than the space between the halves of most hourglasses, and this allows us to shape it in a richer variety of ways. As you blow the glass, you can bend it, spiral it, zigzag it, or keep it straight—give it any number of designs, as long as its contents can move smoothly through it to the other end.

THE PROCESS OF COMPOSITION

The greatest anxiety in writing lies not in trying to write well, but in trying to write anything at all. Breaking the blankness of the page, crossing the divide between abstract thought and actual language, can intimidate even the most practiced writer. How do we do it? What can make it easier?

"Don't let panic cloud your judgment," Diana Roberts Wienbroer et al. counsel to start with in *Rules of Thumb For Business Writers*. They continue, "You can reduce a mountainous, overwhelming project into a series of steps." They then delineate the four basic stages of the writing process that most writers follow:

- "Developing your points and a plan
- Producing a first draft
- Revising—polishing for logic and style
- Editing—fine-tuning for correctness"

"Some writers move step-by-step through each phase of the project," Wienbroer et al. elaborate. "They dislike chaos and prefer to work steadily, spreading the work over the full time available. Other writers, however, get excellent results by putting themselves under last-minute pressure. They thrive on tension and excitement. They often work out of order, moving back and forth, writing different parts and reorganizing as they go." Those who write in this less methodical way tend to fuse the steps of the writing process: they may continue developing their plan while already writing their first draft, or may revise or edit previous parts before finishing a draft. No matter how blended they become in sequence, planning, drafting, revising, and editing make up the essential ingredients that every writer who hopes to succeed must include in composition.

There's something to be said, however, for allowing oneself time to engage in the steps in the order presented above. Wouldn't you rather be able to afford to shift steps when the circumstances of writing require and return to the original step to complete it, not work on multiple steps simultaneously and indiscriminately because of the external pressure of a deadline? "The advantages to procrastination are intensity, concentration, and a sense of adventure," states *Rules of Thumb For Business Writers*. "The disadvantages are well known to all procrastinators and their families." Conversely, "The great advantage of being thorough is that you have time to do a good job." This especially holds true, say Wienbroer et al., for planning before your first draft; investing effort in ascertaining what you want to write ahead of time prevents a lot of struggle and backtracking if trying to do so in the moment of writing. "Time spent before you start writing saves time and energy later."

When beginning a writing project, devote some time to generating ideas and organizing them into a writing plan. It simply makes sense to chart out what you want to do with your subject and material before starting your draft. Writing your plan down protects against the unreliability of memory. Most professionals juggle many projects simultaneously; other tasks might intervene between formulating a writing plan and starting a draft. The careful professional won't run the risk of losing ideas for writing after turning his or her mind elsewhere momentarily.

Back when I was engaged, my fiancée and I had an argument about how best to get from the home of a friend of hers—in a neighborhood of winding, convoluted streets—to the nearest subway station when we had to arrive somewhere else by a certain time. Since we had no idea what the most direct route would be, I insisted on taking the only way we knew, which went partially in the opposite direction but was sure to get us there. My fiancée thought it better to head out blindly in the direction of the subway despite the likelihood that any street we ended up on would eventually turn away from it, getting us lost and costing us more time in the long run. I felt her strategy so poor that I began my journey without her. She ended up following me. Trying to plan the course of your writing in the midst of drafting is like trying to navigate those unfamiliar circuitous streets by dead reckoning: regardless of how auspicious your beginning, you can never know whether your progression of ideas will take you where you need to go. (Any wonder my fiancée and I didn't marry?)

"The most immediate way to begin exploring a topic is also the easiest and most familiar: *talk it over* with others," comment Lunsford and Connors. Wienbroer et al. give some guidelines for this approach: "Ask the person just to listen and not say anything for a few minutes. As you talk, you might jot down points you make. Then ask what came across most vividly." You could also ask your listener for more in-depth feedback about how to organize your material, connections or similarities among the points you make, and possible lines of argument—especially if he or she knows a fair amount about your subject. One potential drawback of relying on discussion to generate ideas, though, is that due to the often specialized nature of business writing, you may have trouble finding someone else with the knowledge level on your subject that you have gained from your research.

Although associated more with creative writing, freewriting can help generate ideas and material for expository writing as well. Just write out all your thoughts about your subject in the order they come to you, without stopping and without concern for organization or correctness. Follow the stream of your consciousness. "If you hit a blank space, write your last word over and over—you'll soon have a new idea," write Wienbroer et al., who particularly advocate freewriting. Afterwards, you can glean the best material, support or elaborate on it as necessary, and give it a more logically coherent order. You don't need to freewrite everything in one sitting: a college classmate of mine frequently sent his advisor short e-mails on the progress of his Honors thesis, and said that they helped him shape the paper itself. Wienbroer et al. remark, "Freewriting works well when your topic is subtle, when you want to write in depth." It gives you room to launch out in any direction as far as you can and to explore any nuance.

"Looping," as both Lunsford and Connors and Wienbroer et al. call it, provides a variation on freewriting; "Find your strongest or most intriguing thought" after freewriting, Lunsford and Connors direct. "This is your 'center of gravity,' which you should summarize in a single sentence; it will become the starting point of your next loop." For that next loop, write the "center of gravity" sentence at the top of the page and freewrite again with it as your starting point. Repeat the process until you have enough ideas and material for your project. Wienbroer et al. add that you can use multiple ideas from each "loop" to start new loops, increasing your raw material exponentially.

Simply listing ideas for your writing can help produce and organize material at a very basic level. Wienbroer et al. suggest listing when you don't have enough time to plan more extensively. After listing all your items, "reread the list, looking for patterns, clusters of interesting ideas, or one central idea," says *The New St. Martin's Handbook*. *Rules of Thumb For Business Writers* further recommends to "start grouping the items on the list. Draw lines connecting examples to the points they illustrate. You may prefer to make a tree with branches and subtopics growing from the appropriate branch."

A common way to make a writing plan similar to Wienbroer et al.'s "tree" list is clustering. Write down one idea for your writing—your topic or thesis, preferably—in one word or phrase and draw a circle around it. Then think of details, examples, or subtopics pertaining to that idea; for each, draw a line out from the circle, write the new idea, and circle it as well. As with looping, this process can be extended as far as necessary. To cluster the previous paragraph, I'd start by writing the word "listing" in the middle of a page and circling it. I'd draw a line from it, write "very basic," and circle that. Then I'd draw a line and circle from "very basic" for "not much time." I'd draw another line out from the original circle and write "group items"; after circling that, I'd draw a line from it for "tree" and circle it. That paragraph was shorter and simpler than most—usually your cluster will have multiple lines coming out of each circle.

You could think of clustering as a relaxed, Type-B-personality version of the granddaddy of all writing plans: the outline. *Rules of Thumb For Business Writers* mentions that some writers "need an outline" specifically. I'm one of them; I tend to be exacting and methodical (in a way that Dr. Freud coined a familiar term for) in most things. If one has the time, an outline is probably the best planning technique because it establishes the sequence of your ideas, shows how they are related to one another, and ranks their importance in relation to one another—none of the other techniques covered do all three. *Rules of Thumb For Business Writers* also notes that since it's thorough and exhaustive, the outline especially helps "when you have many points to include." Keep in mind that an outline doesn't have to mean the formal topic outlines we learned to write in grade school, with Roman numerals, then capital letters, and so on. I often mark points in my outlines with just dashes, bullets, and asterisks.

Take for granted that your first draft will be imperfect. As you write, pay broad attention to the flow of your argument and to paragraph and sentence structure, and search for the most precise words to convey what you mean, but don't get too finicky. "Too much concern about correctness can inhibit your writing, so defer the fear of errors until you have your first draft," Wienbroer et al. say. Your priority in your rough draft should be getting your ideas on paper in the order that makes most sense, with minimal delay from dwelling on details. In *Writing Past Dark*, her guide to the writing experience, writer Bonnie Friedman advises, "Before you get neat, get very, very messy." Hence the term "rough draft."

Wienbroer et al. again emphasize, "Don't get stuck trying to perfect your opening sentence or introductory paragraphs. You can always come back to the introduction once you see how the whole project turns out." Writing English essays in college, often only after finishing the body and knowing the full nature of my argument could I write an introduction.

The above strategy makes creating text appear fairly simple: "... in your first draft, just write until you run out of ideas to explore," declares *The New St. Martin's Handbook*. Realistically, on the other hand, you don't want to burden yourself with too much refining after finishing the draft—you want your first draft to count for more than just an amorphous lump of words that you then must sculpt into a shape appropriate to contain and pour out your message. Business writers worry most about tone and prose rhythm in my experience; they want to sound neither too chatty nor too stilted. Look for the simplest yet most exact vocabulary to express your complete meaning. This may demand words that wouldn't ordinarily come to you in conversation, but they should be recognizable to most generally well-educated readers. Employ a range of different sentence structures and make the mechanics of your sentences only as involved as necessary to treat their ideas and their relation to one another. A sentence can be a Swiss Army knife of different components serving different purposes, but it shouldn't be a cumbersome, excessively intricate Rube Goldberg contraption. Strive simultaneously for grace and for strength.

Rules of Thumb For Business Writers offers two strategies for producing a rough draft that break the process down into steps and resemble the looping technique. First, "In one page, write your ideas—everything you've considered including.... Now, you have a rough draft to work with. Expand each point with explanations or examples." You initially create a template that then frames completing the composition. Or, if you prefer, "A simple technique is just to write one paragraph ... that tells the main ideas you have in mind. Arrange the sentences in a logical and effective sequence. Then copy each sentence from that core paragraph onto its own page and write a paragraph or two to back up each sentence. Now you have a rough draft." Strictly speaking, you don't need to put a page break after each sentence to add to them, but having a set space to fill as you develop your work can psychologically reinforce the piecemeal, building-block nature of this strategy.

Even when you carefully prepare a writing plan beforehand, sometimes you don't realize all the implications of an idea until you formally express it. Notwithstanding the importance of developing a writing plan, remain flexible and willing to follow your writing in whatever new direction it moves. "No matter how thoroughly you may have already explored your topic, you will discover more about it while drafting," *The New St. Martin's Handbook* assures us. "Sometimes these new insights will cause you to turn back—to change your organizational plan, to bring in more information, to approach the subject from a new angle, to rethink the way you appeal to your audience, or even to reconsider your purpose." Doing so much work over again can dishearten and frustrate the writer, but to write effectively you must satisfy the writing's needs more than your own. Lunsford and Connors insist, "If you see that your organizational plan is not working, do not hesitate to alter it. If some information now seems irrelevant, leave it out, even if you went to great lengths to obtain it." Writing teachers and students call this "killing your babies"; just because you like something in your writing doesn't mean it belongs there.

Wienbroer et al. agree that your approach to your project may change drastically while drafting: "Your main point may well shift and change as you write. Often, you will come up with better ideas, and as a result, you may change your emphasis. Be prepared to abandon parts or all of your original plan. Some minor points may now become major points." If you come to a radical change in conceiving your project while drafting, it might be easier to begin the draft anew than to face revising a draft that starts off in one direction and ends up somewhere else entirely. If the change in your ideas is less total, continue with your draft in the interest of keeping the momentum of writing and hold on to your changes as a starting point for revision.

The Elements of Style instructs, "Revising is a part of writing"—the most demanding and the most critical part. A long time ago, someone asked me, "Have you ever written just one draft and said, 'That's it'?" I replied, "No. Nobody's that good." Writing with confidence means, paradoxically, not trusting your initial vision for your work; it means trusting your ability to *find* the best vision for it. Often that can't happen until you've entertained every imaginable option. Writing teacher Michael Degen reminds us in his book *Crafting Expository Argument* that "revision means 're-see,'" to view your draft from your readers' perspective in order to determine whether the writing decisions you have made will best elicit the effect you intend.

To start, look for what writers and writing teachers often call "global" changes: adjustments to major, overall aspects of the work such as argument and structure. Lunsford and Connors offer some suggestions on how to revise for argument or exposition. "Can you identify any confusing leaps from point to point? Do you need to provide additional or stronger transitions?" they ask. Force yourself to ask yourself, "If I hadn't written this, would I know what's going on here?" They also advise, "Be particularly careful to note what kinds of evidence, examples, or good reasons you offer in support of your major points. If some points need more elaboration.... take time to gather more information and do further exploration." Don't leave any steps in the development of your thesis understood; usually they won't be.

When revising globally, also ask yourself, in Lunsford and Connors's words, "What organizational strategies are used?... Are they used effectively? Why or why not?" Make sure that the order in which you treat your topics is the best possible. See if you can rearrange your topics so that some or all of them thematically segué into another. In this section, I discussed argument and content before organization, because what you say often determines how you say it; if I had put the paragraph on organization before the paragraph on content in my rough draft (which I didn't), I would want to change that when revising. Lunsford and Connors suggest outlining your draft after you write to see what, if anything, should be changed organizationally. If you can accurately summarize your composition in the structurally and thematically cohesive scheme of the outline, you should be on the right track. If not, you probably need to expand, adjust, rearrange, or remove something.

For parts of your writing that give you difficulty, Wienbroer et al. recommend that you ask not only "Are they in the right place?" but "Do you really need them?" Beware of what I term "ox-bows." An ox-bow lake is a former stretch of river that became a separate body of water when the river changed course. Similarly, in your writing, a vestigial idea from an earlier conception of your work might remain after you reconceived it, or you may not have been able to develop a point that you thought held equal weight with other points when you planned your draft. In either case, the reader can notice that this idea is detached from the main flow of your writing. You probably should drain it out.

You also want to fit your composition to the expected length, if necessary, when revising. After getting everything you have to say on paper in your first draft, you'll need to trim the piece down in revision most of the time. *Rules of Thumb For Business Writers* frames revision for length in terms of self-interrogation, as is its habit: "How much does your specific reader need or want to know?" This is an easy question to ask, but often a hard one to answer honestly. Wienbroer et al. instruct, "Look for minor information that might bore your reader or distract from the main facts." Pet details are one of the most common "babies" to "kill"—information that the writer finds very interesting but which is tangential to his or her focus.

At times, however, your first draft might fall short of your anticipated length, and you might need to beef it up. When we need to considerably lengthen our writing, *Rules of Thumb For Business Writers* tells us to start on the "global" level: "Adding words or phrases to a report makes it, at most, an inch longer. Adding new points or new examples will make it grow half a page at a time." Then we can try to expand on the "local" level by expressing our points more specifically:

Add details (facts, events that happened, things you can see or hear). Details are the life of good writing. Instead of writing, "Ms. Aznavour is a real team player," write, "Ms. Aznavour worked on the Collins account with four others. I observed how she filled in during a colleague's absence, met the holiday deadline in spite of a delay in shipping, and did all this with good humor."

The "local," small-scale revisions you'll make have to do with style—grammar, word choice, and sentence structure. Previous chapters have dealt with these issues, so I won't repeat here what they say. *Rules of Thumb For Business Writers*'s general advice on revising for style should suffice: "If you get tangled up trying to say something that you consider important, stop and ask yourself, 'What is it I'm trying to say, after all?' Then, say it to yourself in plain English and write it down that way."

Lastly, edit your writing for errors in punctuation, capitalization, and spelling. These are also "local" changes that require close scrutiny. To this end, Wienbroer et al. suggest, "Always put a little distance between the writing of a document and the proofreading of it. Set the project aside—at least for 20 minutes if you can. That way, you'll see it fresh and catch errors you might otherwise have overlooked." We proofread most effectively when we detach ourselves from our writing; if we're too close to it, we might glide over mistakes because we're too used to our work's content.

The Elements of Style notes, "Some writers find that working with a printed copy of the manuscript helps them to visualize the process of change; others prefer to revise entirely on screen." Personally, I much prefer proofreading from a hard copy. I have trouble getting a feel for the writing if I can't literally feel it, plus the glow from the monitor makes my eyes glaze over. "Because the eye is more accustomed to noticing errors on paper, you should print and proofread a draft copy of all important documents before sending them," *Rules of Thumb For Business Writers* explains. Actually, it suggests proofreading on screen first to catch the blatant mistakes, then double-checking on a printout. For a series of short pieces I wrote for my job, I proofread both on screen and on paper—sometimes using one medium first, sometimes the other. I forget why I worked that way, but I usually caught errors the second time around that I missed on my first proofread, regardless of which medium I used first.

Most importantly, proofread intently; don't approach it as a cursory gloss over your finished work. "Assume that you have made unconscious errors and really look for them. Slow down your reading considerably, and actually look at every word," warn Wienbroer et al. Lunsford and Connors recommend, "The best way to catch inadvertent omissions is to proofread carefully, reading each sentence slowly—and aloud." This attitude combines diligence and thoroughness with humility. Don't trust yourself to have written a perfect draft because you caught some mistakes immediately while writing. Those instances of perspicuity were probably the exception rather than the rule; while writing, one's concentration usually focuses inward on the sound of the sentences composed rather than outward on their appearance on the screen or page. Search out every place where a typo might be hiding.

I had a neighbor growing up, an artist named Ben Abramowitz, who was an intellectual mentor of sorts to me. He once told me, "People sometimes say, 'I have an idea, I just can't put it into words.' Without expression, there is no idea." An idea's inadequate expression precludes it from impacting others and renders it worthless. In writing, an idea is only as good as the words applied to it.

We've all heard the Chinese proverb, "A journey of a thousand miles begins with a single step." Hokey, but true. Sometimes we wonder how we can ever get from an incipient idea for writing to a finished composition. The only way is to write one word, then another, one at a time; when you get to the end, go back and add words, subtract them, or improve them, until there's no more you can do.

Part 2: Types of Professional Writing

RÉSUMÉS AND COVER LETTERS

No matter the job, everyone who has ever worked has been a salesperson. The self-employed must sell their services to clients; most of us, though, sell our talent and labor to prospective employers. Our sign in the window, our billboard or commercial is the résumé and cover letter we send to apply for positions. But the mere presence of a sign or advertisement does not in itself attract shoppers to a store, and simply possessing experience, education, training, and skills will not interest employers enough to make them call for an interview. Just as marketing must be designed as appealingly as possible to get customers to buy, a résumé and cover letter must be well-written to start the ball rolling toward a hire.

Many résumés begin, after the name and contact information, with an objective, something along the lines of: "To obtain a challenging position utilizing my current skills and providing the growth and experience to expand them." An objective is by no means obligatory. In many cases they're silly; the vagueness of objectives like the example above gives their grandiose diction a hollow ring. "Most of the time," write Diana Roberts Wienbroer et al. in *Rules of Thumb For Business Writers*, "you can omit the objective because it is implied in your application for that particular job." I have only included an objective in my résumé when the application required it, and rarely look at a résumé's objective when reviewing potential hires.

An objective can help, however, to show your ambition if you do want your foot-in-the-door position to lead to something bigger. As they say about job interviews, "Don't dress for the job you're applying for, dress for the job you want." One of the sample résumés included in *Rules of Thumb For Business Writers* suggests that an objective might be useful for recent graduates or others new to the workforce who don't have much experience to report.

NTC's Business Writer's Handbook, by Arthur H. Bell, comments, "The career objective of the résumé can easily be personalized on each résumé you send out." If you think the occasion of your résumé warrants an objective, make it as concrete as you can. What skills of yours do you want the position to draw on, and how? What growth and experience do you anticipate? How do you expect your skills to grow, and what new skills do you expect to acquire? This will indicate to the hiring manager that you've taken the time to reflect on the job and how you would fit into it, as opposed to blindly sending the same cookie-cutter résumé for every position you want without taking account of each job's specifics. Bell also says one can include an immediate objective and a future objective: "By such short-term/long-term statements, you indicate to your reader that you are realistic about entry-level positions, but that you also have aspirations for more lofty goals."

For each job, list your title, the company or organization you worked for, the city and state where you worked, and the dates you worked there. "If your job had no title, feel free to name the job within the bounds of truth (a recreation job might be titled 'Swimming Instructor,' but not 'Nautical Locomotion Consultant')," advises *Rules of Thumb For Business Writers*. If you were promoted at a company, list each title you held there within a single entry, separated from the others by a semicolon; the entry for one of my bookstore jobs begins, "Clerk; Supervisor; Assistant Manager." If your title change resulted from a shift across departments, however, devote a separate entry to each to clarify the difference in the nature of the positions. In my own résumé, I have one entry for my stint as circulation manager of the Boston *Jewish Advocate* and another entry for my position as administrative assistant and accounts receivable specialist there. Bell recommends a variation from the order I gave above. "If your employment has been steady year by year, emphasize that fact by placing the dates first," he writes. "If, on the other hand, you have had long employment gaps, give the dates less emphasis by placing them after the job listing . . ."

In the sub-points to each entry, describe your duties in that position. This description fleshes out for the reader the nature of the work you did there and gives him or her an idea of its applicability to the position at hand. If your duties were numerous and diverse, selectively list those most relevant to the job you're applying for to keep that entry from lengthening out of control. If I were applying for a promotion to data analyst or project manager at my market research company, I could safely leave out grunt work like boxing up old paper surveys for storage. Furthermore, you could include fewer sub-points for older jobs.

Education is another important résumé section. "Sometimes you may wish to elaborate upon your education experience, perhaps to compensate for limited work experience," writes Bell. "In that case, create meaningful subcategories for EDUCATION:

Degrees
Pertinent Coursework
Awards and Scholarships
Publications
Future Educational Plans ..."

Personally, I think you only need to make your education section this elaborate if you've just finished school and have little real work experience to report, or if the job you want is academic or research-related; I give this level of detail when I send résumés for writing or teaching and tutoring jobs. Otherwise, simply list your degree, the school you received it from, and the dates attended. "While few employers hire on the basis of college grades alone, you should not hesitate to put down a good GPA on your résumé," comments Bell. You can put academic awards and scholarships in a separate honors and awards section. Publications can be made into their own section, or be put with honors and awards. As for mentioning future educational plans, *NTC's Business Writer's Handbook* sees only one side of the issue: "While this category remains optional on your résumé, you should consider its advantages.... If you plan to acquire a new business skill, master another language, or work toward advanced degrees, why not say so?" Because, if you plan to continue your education full-time, it means you might not stick around long enough to make hiring you worthwhile. Including future educational plans might work in applying for entry-level positions that build one's experience before ascending the corporate ladder or others that tend to involve a high level of turnover, because the company already expects that you will move on. For more advanced career-track positions, though, there's no harm in keeping plans to go back to school to yourself.

It often makes sense to include volunteer activities on your résumé as well; *NTC's Business Writer's Handbook* observes, "If you have had virtually no paid work experience at all, list volunteer experiences related to business concerns." But other activities can strengthen your résumé even in conjunction with work experience. If I were interested in a publishing job, for instance, in addition to having checked facts for a client's book at my current job, I would want to mention editing my local writers' group's first anthology and editing poetry for my graduate school's literary magazine. The golden rule of relevance also applies to this section: the instructor of my Advanced Composition class in college told us that if we're applying for an office job we wouldn't include in our résumé that we juggled at the state fair. Ever the wise guy,

I countered, "Unless you have to handle multiple projects at the same time." Nevertheless, you can and may want to interpret relevance more liberally here. I told a friend of mine to note her participation in choir and a drama club on the résumé she sent for a waitressing job (yes, they actually asked for a résumé)—her desire as a performer to please an audience would have stood her in good stead in persuading the restaurant manager that she can provide customers an enjoyable dining experience.

Sections on particular skills—typing speed, computer programs you know, and so forth—and on honors, awards, or publications can round out your résumé.

Once you decide on the information to include in your résumé, think about the order you want to arrange it in. Work experience is usually the most important part of the résumé: start with that. Most people write chronological résumés, presenting prior jobs in the order held. Actually, I advise listing jobs in reverse chronological order, starting with the most recent; your interviewer will be most interested in your immediate background, so he or she should see that first. *NTC's Business Writer's Handbook* refers to a "functional résumé," in which "your most impressive jobs [come] first, your least impressive jobs last.... Let the emphasis fall on the job title and description of your responsibility, rather than upon the dates you held the job ..." This might be a good strategy for people with a wealth of significant work experience. However, I've never seen a résumé of this kind outside of Bell's book; I'd worry that the prospective employer would find a non-chronological résumé too outlandish to know what to make of it.

Generally, I place my education section next. But if your other activities are more germane to the position applied for than the subject you have your degree in, or if your higher education record is incomplete or isn't terribly impressive, put other activities ahead of education. I conclude my résumé with skills—there's not much to say besides what they are—but if your skill set is more substantial than other categories of your résumé, you might want to locate this section earlier.

I had always included my references at the end of my résumé until, a few years ago, a career counselor recommended I leave them out. She explained that all employers expect all applicants to have references; including them in your résumé doesn't impress them and simply lengthens the amount of print on the page. Moreover, most employers don't call references until after the interview, until they know you're seriously worth considering. She suggested instead that I list references on a separate sheet of paper to provide at the interview.

Hiring managers don't read most résumés—they skim them. Usually, the volume of applications received, deadlines to fill jobs, and other duties prevent those in charge of hiring from examining all résumés in-depth; they give each a quick once-over to find those that catch their interest and then look at those few more closely. Therefore, the résumé should have a clean, smooth appearance, enabling the reader to easily pick up information at a glance.

I put my name and contact information at the top center in bold on my own résumé. This is what I really want whoever will read my résumé to remember: who I am and how to reach me to schedule an interview. You might also make the point size of this information larger than that of the rest of the résumé or type your name in all capitals.

Skipping down a line from my personal information, I type my first section heading in bold. If my résumé includes an objective, I make that my first section. Otherwise, I write in roman (normal) type the first job title or achievement accomplished, the company I worked for or the venue of the achievement, the location of the job, and the dates I held the job or the date I accomplished the achievement. I bullet each of these main entries with the wedge-shaped insignia from the bullet menu—I think it's the sleekest, most professional-looking option.

➢ Supervisor, Barnes & Noble College Bookstores, Boston, MA (2000-2002)

Beneath each of these main entries and without skipping a line, I add duties for each job and, if applicable, details of each achievement in italics. I indent them and bullet each one with a regular round bullet.

➢ Supervisor, Barnes & Noble College Bookstores, Boston, MA (2000-2002)

- *Customer service*
- *Assigned tasks*
- *Trained new employees*
- *Received and shelved new books*
- *Ordered books from distributors*
- *Reduced backlog of books to return to distributors*

Items in some sections, such as skills, may not need details. "Typing: 50 words per minute" could suffice. However, if you have received an award for or official recognition of your skill, you may want to list it with achievements instead:

➢ Typing Certificate, Twinklefingers Clerical School, Hoboken, NJ (2003)
- *50 words per minute*

Skip lines between one entry and another, and between entries and section headings. You don't have to use boldface and italics the same way I do; you might just vary the point size among headings, entries, and details instead of varying the typeface. Arrange the information in a consistent pattern, as in an outline, so the reader will know from a piece of information's position and appearance on the page what kind of information it is: a section heading, a main entry, or the detail of an entry. At the same time, distinguish each kind of information typographically so that, in the course of reading, your audience will know whether you are moving from a major category of information to a subcategory or are changing categories.

§

Everyone should know two things about cover letters going into writing one. First, as *NTC's Business Writer's Handbook* says, "The letter should not try to outdo or redo the résumé itself.... Instead, select one or two of your most impressive or interesting achievements and weave them smoothly into the application letter ..." The cover letter serves to expand on the most important items in your résumé, to spell out the significance to the available position that their inclusion in the résumé implies.

Second, focus on you, not them. As a teenager, I had the audacity and naïveté to hit up my county's weekly newspaper for a job as a cub reporter. I had a writer friend in his twenties to whom I showed my cover letter for advice. In the first paragraph, I wrote about what a great newspaper the Prince George's *Journal* was, what an important function it served, and how much I liked to read it—I really laid it on thick. My friend pointed out that this was a mistake. The audience of your cover letter already knows about the qualities of his or her organization; the kind of junk I had written evades the point. Your audience wants to read about your qualities and why you think they make you compatible with his or her organization. (I didn't get the job, but I'm sure that was due to my inexperience, not to my revision of the cover letter.)

Wienbroer et al. include a sample cover letter at the end of *Rules of Thumb For Business Writers*. Don't use it. It jumbles the writer's skills, experience, and attitude toward the job throughout with no trace of method or rationale; letters like theirs won't impress your interviewer with your organizational skills. Cover one aspect of your pitch at a time.

Regarding the visual layout of your cover letter on the page, refer to the business letter format protocols mentioned in the next chapter.

In your cover letter's first paragraph, declare your application for the position. Mention the title of the position and, for a position that you know is available, how you learned of it: "I am writing to apply for the position of dogcatcher that I saw advertised on www.meniallabor.com." They could have advertised other positions, and could have advertised each type of position in a different place. You could be doing them a favor by informing them of why you're writing and where you're coming from, while additionally providing feedback on which advertising markets produce the best results. Besides, specificity is always more helpful and more professional than not. *Rules of Thumb For Business Writers* counsels, "If you have a personal connection, mention it up front (and do everything possible to find a personal connection)." If you have a friend who works for the prospective employer already, mention that fact in your first paragraph, even if he or she didn't tell you about the job—it shows that you're somewhat familiar with the company or organization, which could contribute to predisposing your audience in your favor.

What if you're making a cold inquiry, proposing a job for yourself even though your audience hasn't advertised such a position, as I did with the *Journal*? Bell writes, "You begin, therefore, by referring to common interests, a recent company development, or a topic sure to arouse the curiosity of the reader." Present some kind of motive or pretext for asking your audience to hire you so you don't sound like some desperate weirdo sending job inquiries everywhere and anywhere; when the employer isn't looking for people, you must argue even harder that hiring you would be worth their while. Understandably, personal connections would be even more important.

Now that you've announced the occasion for the letter, in your second paragraph explain why you would excel in the position. Refer to and elaborate on a few items from your résumé to illustrate what you can bring to the table. Research the company you're applying to beforehand; Wienbroer et al. advise, "Stress how you will fit into this particular organization." Demonstrate how your skills and experience match the company's focus—or how they complement the company's focus and can expand it into new, related, and useful areas.

In your third paragraph, explain why you want the job and what you hope to get out of it. You could cite professional reasons like career growth and advancement, acquiring additional or different experience and skills, the desire to work with the specific company offering the job or its type of company, and the like. You could cite personal reasons like the significance to you of the kind of work you would do or that the company does, your interest in or commitment to certain issues involved in the job, or how the job fits your personality. Or both. Convince your reader in this paragraph that you're genuinely interested in *this* job, not just *a* job; show him or her what attracts you to the position and what will drive you to perform if you get it.

Your fourth and final paragraph will be short like your first. Usually it only needs to consist of a complimentary close like "Please find my résumé enclosed. Thank you for considering my application. I look forward to your response." *NTC's Business Writer's Handbook* additionally suggests,

> In the final paragraph of the uninvited letter of application, consider leaving the door open for something less than a formal job interview. If a company presently has no openings, the manager may still wish to meet with you to consider you for future positions. Make it clear that you would be happy to visit with him or her, even if there are no current openings.

This strategy could create a continuing relationship, which will keep you in the hiring manager's mind until you do arrange an interview.

As for the closing, no word could possibly sound more insincere than "Sincerely." Try "Respectfully" or, especially if there is a personal connection with the reader or company, "Cordially."

A résumé and a cover letter themselves won't land you a job, but rarely will you land one worth having without them—or without good ones. They open the door to the interview, where the prospective employer takes your full measure. Thus, the résumé and cover letter make your first impression on the employer; the analogy of "dressing for the job you want" that I used specifically about the résumé objective applies to the résumé and cover letter in general. Someone showing up for an interview in wrinkled, slovenly clothes would probably make a job interviewer wonder how he or she takes care of himself or herself, not to mention how they would attend to the company's work. Someone wearing neat, crisp, trim clothes, on the other hand, projects competence and orderliness. Similarly, an effectively written résumé and cover letter indicate that you can think creatively and analytically and can present and organize information to achieve a purpose much more than a slipshod résumé and cover letter do. To a hiring manager, they make you worth pursuing.

BUSINESS CORRESPONDENCE

Good communication plays a vital role in business relationships; to make them work, vendor and customer must have a clear understanding of products or services offered and chosen and of the other party's needs, demands, and expectations. Spoken communication can suffice for quick transactions, but most large projects involving a significant amount of time require written correspondence to effectively convey their important details.

In *Rules of Thumb For Business Writers*, Diana Roberts Wienbroer et al. write,

> Most business writers send out a few standard letters—over and over. There are templates (providing design and layout) in most word-processing programs—and even letters to copy. Unfortunately, the rest of the business world has access to those same standard letters. If you develop your own templates, including key sentences, all you'll have to do is change a few details for a personalized letter.

Letter templates save a great deal of labor; I use them myself in replying to respondent inquiries about my company's surveys. At the same time, we all like to be acknowledged as individuals. I remember how surprised and gratified I felt reading a reply from Senator Barbara Mikulski to a letter I wrote to her, in which she addressed the specific points I raised—showing that she herself had read my letter with interest. This is all the more true, because less expected, when the writer represents a corporate entity rather than his or her personal interests.

To balance the demands of convenience and of personalization, create your own templates as Wienbroer et al. mention—one for each type of letter you send. If a new situation for sending letters starts occurring more frequently, make a template for it. When adjusting the template to write a letter, refer (however briefly) to specific aspects of the recipient's situation to demonstrate concern for serving his or her individual needs. The letter template should serve as a model to vary and improvise from, not a mold that all correspondence must fit into.

As for layout, most business letters adhere to certain standard protocols. The usual format for business letters is called modified block style, and it's the format I like best. Everything is typed single-spaced. The writer's address (which may not be necessary if using company letterhead) and the date are typed at the top of the page, indented to the number 4 on the screen's ruler bar.

1234 Main Street
Bozotown, MA 98765
December 1, 2008

Skip a line, and then type the recipient's name, title if any, the company name if applicable, and the address starting at the left margin; skip another line and type the greeting, ending with a colon.

Jonathan Hind
Human Resource Manager
Doofus Bowlingpin-Setting Company
0001 Rockfish Lane
Moronia, MD 22222

Dear Mr. Hind:

Skip a line before starting the body of the letter. Don't indent the first lines of paragraphs—instead, indicate separation of paragraphs by keeping a blank line between them. After the last paragraph, skip a line and type the closing from the number 4 on the ruler bar, ending with a comma. Drop down four lines to accommodate your handwritten signature after you print the letter and type your name starting from the number 4 on the ruler bar (if sending the letter by e-mail, dispense with the extra signature space). This format balances the type on the page and thus pleases the eyes: your address, the date, the closing, and your signature on the right side of the page visually counterpoint the recipient's name and address, the greeting, and the body justified to the left. Block style, the other common business letter format, in which every part of the letter begins flush left, looks lopsided and—because your address and the date appear directly above the addressee's name, title, and address—top-heavy.

If you have only a title for your addressee and no name, or only a first name, begin with the title. For the greeting, however, you can still be somewhat personal with an anonymous audience. "Dear Sir or Madam" at least expresses some interest in relating to the reader as an individual and is more cordial than "Dear Acme Company" or the overused "To Whom It May Concern." This greeting also works well when the contact's gender is obscured by their use of initials or of a unisex name like Leslie, Chris, or the legendary Pat.

"Usually a letter contains two or more paragraphs," Wienbroer et al. write. A business letter frequently conveys important information or relates to an important situation; its body should have an appropriately substantial length. Nonetheless, a letter should not aspire to the detail and exhaustiveness of a report—rarely should a business letter exceed one typed page. Wienbroer et al. also recommend making your paragraphs brief, allowing your reader to digest their contents quickly and easily.

They continue, "BEGIN WITH THE PURPOSE OF YOUR LETTER." The first sentence of the body of the letter, which can also function as its first paragraph, should most often straightforwardly state your reason for communicating:

"I am writing to report about the employment history of Ms. Carrie Young.
Thank you for a very informative tour of your facilities.
This letter is a formal request for a change in the packaging you use for our mushrooms."

Beginning with the point will enhance ease of reading. After all, this is the most important thing your letter has to say. Business letters tend to be primarily expository, and the "inverted pyramid" structure of the newspaper article (pure expository writing *par excellence*) places the most important facts first. Your reader will likely be a busy person with many duties to perform and therefore will not want you to unnecessarily delay your declaration of intent.

Some people complain that the ease and casualness of e-mail has led to a decline in the art of letter-writing. One shouldn't let the speed of delivery provided by electronic communication persuade one that speed—which usually results in laxity—of composition fits this medium in formal circumstances. Regardless of the medium, your correspondence should always be in top form when business is on the line: take the time to put it in top form.

Sales letters are probably the most common in the business world. When pitching your company's products or services to another company, Arthur H. Bell in *NTC's Business Writer's Handbook* suggests the following organizational model:

S—Spark the imagination early in the letter.
A—Announce what you have to say or sell
L—List its benefits or features.
E—Express appreciation for the reader's interest.
S—Specify what you want the reader to do.

In general, each section of the letter opens a deeper level of information to the reader than the previous section—although I would reverse the last two steps. Expressing appreciation after specifying the desired action exerts the subtle pressure of courtesy on the reader to perform that action. The first section violates the general guideline of stating a letter's purpose at its start for good reason: it tantalizes the reader with an alluring aspect of what you have to sell. To use this strategy successfully, research your audience and mention something specifically relevant to its business or interests to "spark the imagination." The reader will likely be positively inclined to do business with you because the familiarity with your audience that your letter demonstrates implies that you will understand your reader's needs and limitations and build a distinctive rapport. *NTC's Business Writer's Handbook* explains, "'What I'm selling,' the writer seems to say to the reader, 'isn't just good. It's good for *you*.'"

Bell discusses some of these steps a bit more in depth regarding the direct mail sales letter. Soliciting business from individuals by letter is no longer very common in the days of the Internet and the bulk mail catalog, but it's still a vital tool for raising money in the non-profit sector (I myself became a member of Amnesty International and The Humane Society through direct mail). Bell mentions several ways to provide the attention-catching introduction, the "hook":

1. Suggest . . . that you can do something unique for the reader:
   Lebanon Tire Company offers you a new way to....
2. Drop an impressive or familiar name, then associate the reader with that name:
   Astronaut Luke Seaboy, like you, knows the importance of regular eye examinations.
3. Mention local people, places, and events:
   Hinton, Iowa, had dirt streets twenty years ago when my father built the Welco Drug Store....
4. Empathize with your reader:
   Cash emergencies occasionally catch us all off guard, especially as the holidays near.
5. Offer something free or at a large discount:
   We want to send you a portable television in exchange for an hour or your time.

Numbers 2, 3, and 4 correspond to the *S* level of Bell's general sales letter plan. They grab the reader's interest through recognition: the reader recognizes parts of his or her daily life mentioned, and is propelled onward through the letter by a sense of fellow-feeling. Numbers 1 and 5 operate by relation, hinting that you understand the reader's needs or wants by offering something you expect the reader to find advantageous. They combine the *S* and *A* levels of Bell's plan, presenting what you have to offer and simultaneously intriguing the reader with it.

"The body of the letter must deliver its message in an efficient, readable, high-interest fashion," proclaims Bell. "Short paragraphs, highlighted words, and frequent headings keep the reading experience lively and persuasive." These aides to readability come in especially handy when your offer is complex or elaborate. Lastly, "the direct mail letter ends with a specific call for action: mail the return card, call the 800 number, check the 'yes' box, and so forth." Spell out the required action on the reader's part clearly, and use ease of doing business to win over the reader by making this action as simple as possible.

Another prevalent genre of business correspondence is the adjustment letter—responding to a customer's request for money back or a credit to his or her account. Probably someone else will make the decision on the customer's request, but *NTC's Business Writer's Handbook* presents four things to consider before writing an adjustment letter:

- "Is the customer right?
- Is the problem the company's fault?
- Can I admit that fault?
- Can I resolve the problem satisfactorily?"

The positive (from the customer's perspective) adjustment letter is easy enough. In keeping with the principle of opening with your letter's purpose, Bell writes, "Begin the response by promptly disclosing the good news: 'Yes, this company grants your claim.' Be sure to restate the claim in brief form ..." Summarizing the claim will heighten the customer's satisfaction with the resolution by indicating that your company fully understands the problem. Bell goes on, "Necessary details are provided later in the letter, often in the second paragraph." These could include why you're granting the adjustment—the circumstances, evidence, or policies that led you to judge in the customer's favor—and whether the adjustment will be made by cash back, store credit, account credit, etc. "The writer tries to restore goodwill and customer satisfaction at the end of the letter," Bell concludes. He or she can say that the company looks forward to continuing doing business with the customer and assure the reader of his or her value as a customer, and can affirm the company's commitment to strive for the highest level of quality and fairness. The sample positive adjustment letter included in *NTC's Business Writer's Handbook* also provides contact information in its conclusion in case of further issues and cross-sells the reader on other products the reader may find interesting.

Writing the negative adjustment letter, however, requires delicacy. *NTC's Business Writer's Handbook* advises, "Maintain a professional, even tone in your response." Remember that no matter how obnoxious or belligerent the customer may be, the matter is not personal. Bell warns, "Take care not to use language that may cause you or your company future problems. In particular, beware of admitting company responsibility or liability unless you have authorization for such statements."

In terms of structure, the elements of the negative adjustment letter resemble those of the positive adjustment letter, but in different order. *NTC's Business Writer's Handbook* relates, "The form of the negative adjustment letter usually follows three stages. First, let the reader know that you understand the nature of his or her complaint and have looked into the matter in appropriate ways." To this end, Bell recommends, "Assess the justice of the claim without bias. Make an honest effort to see the situation from the client's point of view." This will persuade the customer that your company is not acting out of sheer selfishness or unconcern. "Second, set forth your decision firmly and politely. Finally, give whatever explanation or interpretation you feel is appropriate, concluding with a statement of goodwill." I would reverse the order of the second and third stages, retracing for the customer the reasoning behind your decision in order to lead up to announcing the decision itself; if the customer can first follow your logic in making the decision, you might have a better chance of him or her accepting that decision once your letter arrives at it. While that defers stating the purpose of the letter until nearly the end, that's a good place for news that the reader doesn't want to hear.

You could use statements of goodwill similar to those I suggested for the positive adjustment letter. *NTC's Business Writer's Handbook*'s sample negative adjustment letter emphasizes closing on a constructive note, saying what you can do for the reader instead of an adjustment or politely noting what the reader can do to avoid the problem in the future (especially if he or she could have done this but ignored it). Bell stresses that business writing should employ positive language over negative whenever possible:

> Business communicators.... can choose to write what can be done (the positive approach) or opt to state what can't be done (the negative approach):
> POSITIVE: Please fill out the remaining blank lines on the application and return it to us as soon as possible.
> NEGATIVE: You failed to fill out the application completely. We cannot take action of any kind until you have completed the form appropriately.

Granted, avoiding negative language when writing to tell someone that you will not do something poses a challenge. Perhaps the statement of denying the adjustment could be replaced or immediately followed by "To make up for the confusion over the status of your account, we would be happy to provide you a mattress free of charge" or "To prevent further confusion regarding your account, please note on each check the number of the invoice it is intended to pay." Bell elaborates, "The reason for such caution goes beyond common courtesy and politeness to an understanding of motivation and persuasion. Your audience is much more likely to act as you wish"—or, in this case, accept your action—"if not put off by excessively negative language."

The claims letter responds to a customer's complaint about a product's failure or malfunction; it's similar to the adjustment letter, but the claims letter may have nothing to do with bookkeeping, and the adjustment letter may have nothing to do with quality of merchandise. Its procedure is essentially the same as that of the adjustment letter, although Bell gives it its own nifty little mnemonic acronym: ACTION. Before writing, he says,

> "A – Assess the whole situation. . . .
> C – Calm down. Few persuasive 'action' letters are written in the heat of anger."

If a claim or customer gets you really riled up, take a page (no pun intended) from the character Yolek Lifshitz in the Israeli writer Amos Oz's novel *A Perfect Peace*. Yolek is the secretary of a *kibbutz* and a political big shot. Whenever he has to write a letter to someone he's angry at, he produces a long, vituperative tirade that, as soon as he finishes, he crumples up and throws in the trash. Having discharged the emotional electricity within himself, he then writes a much shorter, more polite and restrained version, which he actually sends.

In the letter itself,

"T – Tell what happened. . . .

   I – Insist on a defined action to remedy the situation. . . .

   O – Offer cooperation. . . .

   N – Name a specific step the reader should take to begin remedying the problem."

I'm not fully clear on this, but I assume Step *I* represents the overall course of action, which is broken down into the company's action in Step *O* and the customer's action in Step *N*.

   NTC's Business Writer's Handbook suggests empathizing with the reader, especially if the product or service caused physical or property damage. Its sample claims letter additionally notes the consequences of not taking the action requested in the letter. This could mean forfeiture of the claim, willingness to face the customer in court if he or she has threatened to sue—but again, confirm that your company authorizes you to say that—or something else, depending on the nature of the individual claim.

   Occasionally the tables turn, and you may have to write to a vendor to make a claim or argue for an adjustment. In your first paragraph, as usual, declare the issue at hand. The second paragraph should recount the history of what went wrong in this incident and how and why it went wrong. Next, state specifically how you would like the vendor to rectify the problem: money back, account credit, product replacement, or Super Bowl tickets (well, it's worth a shot). There's no need to beat around the bush in your request. *Rules of Thumb For Business Writers* affirms, "If you expect a particular outcome as a response to your letter, say so—politely, but up front. Use *I* and *you*.

   I expect your company to replace the entire 6/7/00 shipment, which was damaged because of your driver's negligence."

In my opinion, "I expect" sounds slightly too aggressive; I'd recommend "I would like ..." or "I would appreciate your company replacing ..." Even if every principle of sound business entitles you to expect that your audience follow through with your proposed course of action, they will be more positively inclined toward it if you phrase it as a request and not a demand.

   Close the letter with contact information, thanks for your reader's consideration, and a note of goodwill—leverage guilt and the power of suggestion by expressing your confidence that your reader will correct the situation and preserve your positive relationship. Ending on an amicable note reinforces that your letter doesn't call into question your reader's competence or integrity (unless blatantly called for) but simply alerts him or her of a problem to fix. If your audience doesn't feel put off by your letter, they won't put you off.

   Memoranda are somewhat less formal communications usually sent internally within an organization, although clients with whom you work closely may also be included in the audience. Whereas letters tend to relate to single, unique occasions, memos mainly concern progress or new developments in an ongoing situation.

   Begin with the classic memo heading: the "TO:" line containing the names of the recipients (and, optionally, a "CC:" line for people you aren't directly writing to but whom you would like to know what's going on), the "FROM:" line containing your name, and the "RE:" line announcing the memo's subject. Wienbroer et al. point out, "If you have written your subject line accurately, the rest of the memo need be only briefly informative or persuasive."

As a result, memos tend to be shorter than letters, sometimes as short as one paragraph; since your recipients already generally know about your subject, you won't have to recapitulate its background much. Wienbroer et al. also advise, "If your message is complicated, use bullets or headings to break out key points"—which their sample memo does, even though its message isn't complicated. The relative informality of the memo allows you to take these liberties with its graphic layout on the page, making it akin to a text slide in a PowerPoint presentation. Also because of the memo's lesser formality, "Do not use a complimentary close—as with a letter. You may use a brief closing remark as a conclusion."

I've come across various structural models for memos, all of them feasible. The most basic, and the one most like the business letter, is presented by Bell in *NTC's Business Writer's Handbook*:

"The main message
↓
Interpretation or additional information
↓
Action taken or requested"

Bell also offers a pattern specifically for information about a change. He calls it

Pattern A: Situation/Complication/Resolution
Paragraph 1: What is the current situation or past situation?
Paragraph 2: What problem or complication has arisen or may arise?
Paragraph 3: How can the problem be resolved? What should be done?

One of *Rules of Thumb For Business Writers*'s sample memos roughly illustrates this pattern, with extra paragraphs, regarding bad news: a layoff announcement resulting from a merger. The first paragraph informs the reader of the staff reduction. The second presents the reasons for the reduction; the third gives more detail on how the reduction will be made. The fourth paragraph announces ways in which the company will help those laid off deal with the consequences. The last paragraph reads, "We very much regret the hardship this reduction will entail. However, a reinvigorated DellMore within ISF will ultimately bring the greatest benefit to the greatest number of our employees." The memo does its best to close on a note of consolation, offering sympathy and the lukewarm comfort that more people will benefit from this decision than suffer.

Lastly, Wienbroer et al. include a sample of a purely informational memo, which requires no action of the recipient. It is organized along the "inverted pyramid" model mentioned before, in which each succeeding part presents a narrower and less essential level of detail. The first paragraph of the memo, about a new stock option plan for employees, is written like a news lead, presenting the fundamental who, what, where, when, why, and how of the subject. The paragraph after gives an overview of how the stock option plan will work. The third and fourth paragraphs detail the plan's restrictions, and the fifth explains which employees are eligible. The sixth paragraph announces who's in charge of administering the plan so that readers know whom to contact if they want more information.

Wienbroer et al. comment that, curiously, while the writing situation of the memo is less formal than that of the business letter, "Memos can range in tone from the very formal to the casual, but they are almost always more impersonal than a letter. Whenever you need to communicate any kind of sensitive or confidential information, use a letter instead of a memo." Memos have more of the flavor of the office. They are official, organizational communications: their recipients know they receive them because of their place in or continuing relationship with the organization. Letters written to customers usually involve a single interaction or situation; even if it is one of many interactions between them over their history, the customer often expects the company to think of him or her as a private entity interacting with the company at this particular point of contact, not as defined by his or her relationship with the company. Moreover, memos also often have several recipients—perhaps even an entire company— whereas letters are written customarily to one person. For all these reasons, letters commend themselves to bearing more of a personal touch, and memos suit themselves more to mass communication.

NEWSLETTERS AND PRESS RELEASES

"Newsletters are increasing in number and popularity each year as a way for companies to communicate internally and externally," remarks Arthur H. Bell in *NTC's Business Writer's Handbook*. Company newsletters offer a way to highlight activities and accomplishments to your whole organization—and beyond. Diana Roberts Wienbroer et al., authors of *Rules of Thumb For Business Writers*, explain, "Newsletters can serve as great promotional tools outside the company; in-house, they can inform, entertain, and encourage camaraderie." In addition, businesses often issue press releases to inform external audiences of current developments. Newsletters and press releases resemble most types of business writing in that the organization's operation provides their content, but their journalistic form differs vastly from that of the common office report. This chapter will guide you through the basics of corporate journalism.

Hard news articles will form the staple of your organization's newsletter. As you probably already know by living in our media-saturated society, the lead, or first paragraph, of the news story should tell "who," "what," "where," "when," "why," and "how" about your story. "Tell the heart of the story first," Bell insists. *Rules of Thumb For Business Writers* gives an example of a typical news lead:

"On May 23, 2000, Mergentine broke ground for its new headquarters in Amarillo."

Occasionally, however, you may want to use a "grabber"—a less workmanlike, more creative and surprising lead for articles on especially momentous or unusual topics, approaching them from an unconventional angle. We could recast *Rules of Thumb For Business Writers*'s example above as a grabber like this: "The course of Mergentine's future lies in a shovelful of dirt." The take, or second paragraph, would then deliver the more hard-and-fast essential facts.

Journalists often describe the structure of the news article as an "inverted pyramid," meaning that the story gives the most important information in its briefest and most basic form first, then unfolds its supporting information in detail. But don't let the term "inverted pyramid" trick you. Although the information related in the body of your news article should be less generally or broadly important than that in the lead, it should be fuller in incidental detail to flesh out the lead's synopsis of the story. The body of the hypothetical article about Mergentine's new headquarters could cover the projected opening date, specifics about the new building (size, amenities), why the company needs it, and its expected impact on the company. News articles rarely have formal conclusions: they often end with a minor fact or an illustrative quote.

Besides structure, news articles differ from standard business writing in style: "Keep paragraphs and sentences short for easy reading," says *NTC's Business Writer's Handbook*. The usual guideline of varying sentence and paragraph length normally doesn't apply to news writing. Most newspaper articles are written to a fifth-grade reading level; their uniform brevity of expression allows their contents to be easily grasped by anyone, regardless of education level. While you yourself might be surrounded by professionals with advanced degrees in your office, consider whether your company employs considerable numbers of blue-collar workers as well when writing for its newsletter. Moreover, since newsletter pieces tend to be shorter and more general in focus than project reports, their ideas are usually less complex and thus don't require as many complex sentences.

Interviews supply much of the raw material of news articles. Prepare a list of questions beforehand, but anticipate asking new questions and following new lines of thought as a result of the interviewee's responses. Secondary research in written sources also plays an important part in journalism; here, too, the journalist should be open to the unexpected. When I was in high school an older friend and neighbor of mine, a working writer, wanted to hire me as a research assistant for a book he planned about his family's history.

"Say you found the name of the town in Poland where they lived," he quizzed me. "What would you do?"

"Well, I'd look for more information about that town," I said. Common sense, but it indicates that journalists should follow each trail of information as far as it goes—then turn in a new direction and pick up another. If they didn't have deadlines, journalists would never finish anything.

"Quote authoritative sources," Bell instructs, "and refer to facts, not impressions." In college I read an article in the campus Jewish newspaper about Jews for Jesus—negatively slanted, as one might expect—based almost entirely on comments by the rabbi who directed the university's Hillel House. While the reporter described the various promotional paraphernalia displayed in the front windows of the organization's local headquarters, no contact was made with Jews for Jesus or any of its members. Entering the headquarters would be forbidden by Jewish law if the group used it for worship, but the reporter could have requested an interview at another location or by telephone. Consequently, while the article said a lot, it contained no real information about Jews for Jesus. By contrast, several years later my city's Jewish weekly published an article by a rabbi who attended a Jews for Jesus regional conference. His article also made no pretense of impartiality, but because he founded his criticism on things said by Jews for Jesus about Jews for Jesus, it came across as both fairer and more informative.

That said, Bell also cautions, "Avoid editorializing …" Opinion may have some place in journalism written for general outlets like newspapers and magazines, but seldom is appropriate in organizational newsletters. They function less as forums for public debate than as vehicles for presenting the organization to readers within and without. Like it or not, company newsletters aren't the free press; they're writing for The Man.

You don't have to use all the information you learn when researching. If a fact isn't relevant to your fellow employees, doesn't help capture the nature of your subject, or doesn't fit into the thematic shape of your article, leave it out. *NTC's Business Writer's Handbook* advises, "Focus on high-interest aspects of the story."

Feature articles—profiles of certain people, groups, or things—lend extra flavor to your publication. Wienbroer et al. recommend, "Always include a 'spotlight' story—a case history about a product or application or a feature on different individuals within the organization." Such regular columns attract readers: your co-workers will be curious to learn who will be showcased next.

For shorter feature articles or articles in smaller, no-frills newsletters, a conventional news lead will suffice. While I worked at the art library during college, I wrote an article about our new circulation manager for an edition of the library newsletter (the only edition I remember being published in my four years there). Because the newsletter was only a few pages, and her hire didn't presage a watershed in the library's operation, I began the article with a simple lead answering the Six Primal Questions of Journalism and avoided making it fancier than the material called for.

Nonetheless, you'll probably use grabbers more often for leads of feature stories than of news stories. Because their subject matter tends to be more colorful, their style tends to be more colorful; editors grant feature articles more license for varied, and longer, sentences and paragraphs. But they won't let this license be stretched to its extreme. No paragraph in a newsletter article should take up more than half of a full page's column length.

Here's my best example of a grabber I wrote to introduce a feature article: in the early days of my hometown's writers' group, I wrote an article about us for the local newspaper. The oddest fact about the group was that at that time a police station afforded the only public space we could secure for our monthly open readings. Based on this fact, and on what some might call the sinister appearance of a friend of mine who frequently read—long hair, stocky, an occasional sidelong smirk—I described him standing in the front of the room in the police station as though he might be a newly arrested suspect being arraigned. Then, in the take, I explained what was really happening.

Organize the body of a feature article with a conventional lead using the inverted pyramid. My article about the art library's circulation manager told about her previous positions and experience in the university library system (the information most relevant to her new job), her educational background in India where she was born, comments by the head librarian about her arrival, and other personal information. Feature articles beginning with grabbers tend to be structured like diamonds instead of upside-down pyramids: after explaining the lead the article's focus broadens into an overview of the subject's fundamental information, then narrows like a news story into more specific details. My article about my writers' group continued from the take to describe the purpose and summarize the history of the group. I informed the reader of how the group had grown from the cluster of founding members to its present size. I stated that we held open readings like the one described, as well as general and steering committee meetings, every month; I mentioned future projects the group planned, like publishing an anthology of members' work and finding a less laughable venue for readings. Lastly, I included input from members about the group and reaction to the reading from other attendees.

Product or service profiles can be organized similarly. You can begin with a general description or, in the case of a service or department profile, a "slice of life" vignette capturing the group's atmosphere. Describe the product or service's purpose and its place or role within the company; relate its history or background. Introduce the reader to those who work on it. Conclude with reaction to the product or service from customers and remarks from employees about its significance.

Keep in mind a few general points when writing newsletter articles, whether news or feature. Don't forget that customers, vendors, or shareholders might read the newsletter; make your article accessible enough for a non-employee audience to follow. Wienbroer et al. offer a few steps to take toward this end:

- "Check articles for context and tone—for example, outsiders may not get your 'in' jokes.
- Provide background information when necessary for outsiders.
- Identify all persons by full title or job description."

Also, be conscious of the demands of the newsletter's layout on your writing. Articles have to fit the dimensions of the formatted printed page and fill the length and width of the column space in the section of the page allotted to it. The size constraints common in other types of business writing gain a dimension in publications, becoming space constraints. (Those who write presentations or reports in PowerPoint may have experienced this when dividing a slide into multiple text boxes and trying to make them all the same length.) If you're left with extra space after your article is formatted in the layout template your newsletter uses, you might need to suspend the customary preference for conciseness and add words, sentences, or even a paragraph or two to fill in the vacant column-inches. Add this material in places where ideas could use elaboration, though—it shouldn't look like verbal padding. Conversely, pare away verbiage where possible if your article runs over the space slated for it. Formatting can thus affect your style as much as subject matter. Many newsletter writers compose directly into the layout template to adjust their writing to the publication's spatial demands as they proceed.

Press releases, formal announcements sent to news publications about company developments, represent another form of corporate journalism. While information-driven like the company newsletter article, the press release by definition is written for an external audience; therefore the element of enhancing the company's image and profile is more overt.

Overall, the press release resembles the news article in structure and style, but perhaps in a more boiled-down form: a press release should usually be less than two full typed pages. *Rules of Thumb For Business Writers* contains a sample press release that resembles a formal memorandum, with the addition of more in-depth, defined information on results or impact of the action taken and specifically who it affects or would interest. The book also lists some ingredients of a good press release:

- Use the news lead—*who, what, when, where, how,* and sometimes *why.*
- Be brief. Editors may cut your last few paragraphs, so be sure the important information is up front....
- Identify all individuals by title or position.
- Provide background information and label it as such.
- Provide a press kit, if appropriate ...

My experience confirms the importance Wienbroer et al. place on lean language; when I worked for my hometown newspaper (the same one I wrote the writers' group article for), we were forever trimming inessential text out of press releases. Providing section headings, which Wienbroer et al. hint at, can help an editor identify the most important material, and might persuade him or her that enough thought and planning went into the press release's writing and organization that it's worthy to survive the editorial process intact. You don't need a press kit unless you want the publication to write a longer article on the press release's subject, however. If so, mention this in a cover letter along with the release and kit.

Newsletters and press releases fulfill a dual function of disseminating information and promoting the organization to both internal and external audiences. Corporate journalism alerts employees to goings-on in other parts of the company and in the company as a whole—in the process fostering a sense of belonging, unity, and inclusion and investment in the company's endeavors. For outside readers, corporate journalism clues them in on the kinds of developments to expect from your company, on its position in its industry and market. Presuming this information is positive or can be cast in a positive light, it can boost sales and even, for publicly traded companies, stock value. Newsletters and press releases furnish examples of the vital role of information and its presentation through writing in a competitive economy.

DESCRIPTIVE BUSINESS WRITING

Description is the meat of good writing. Illustrating or evoking something's essence or qualities, creating a picture in the reader's mind with words, lies at the heart of verbal communication. Most kinds of writing employ description, but it constitutes the main purpose of certain types of business writing. This chapter will focus on four types in particular: job descriptions, employee performance reviews, recommendations, and instructions or directions. One could argue that performance reviews and recommendations fall more into the category of persuasive writing, but their persuasion rests predominantly on their description of the subject's accomplishments and abilities rather than on the logical structure of an argument.

The job description, obviously, is the type of business writing in which description plays the most major role. Since the job description is usually used externally for want ads, it should be as clear and informative as possible within its space constraints—it's often someone's first glimpse into your company. *NTC's Business Writer's Handbook*, by Arthur H. Bell, provides an outline for organizing job descriptions:

1. Specify the job title, including any company codes or level numbers.
2. Name the work group, including location, for the job.
3. Give the reporting order for the position.
4. Describe supervisory responsibilities of the job, including the number of employees supervised and their jobs.
5. Provide a list of specific tasks assigned to the job.
6. Describe general responsibilities not covered in the list of specific tasks.
7. Specify prerequisites for the position, including requirements with regard to education and experience.

Bell also gives some tips for describing the activities mentioned in points 4 through 6. "In your list of tasks and responsibilities," he writes, "prefer observable descriptions of these duties:

NOT: maintain regular communication with senior management
INSTEAD: produce a weekly report for senior management."

The better the reader's understanding of exactly what he or she is getting into, the better your chances of getting applicants interested in exactly what this position entails. In addition, Bell directs, "Emphasize actions taken ... rather than results expected:

NOT: responsible for monthly staff meetings
INSTEAD: plans monthly staff meetings."

The former phrasing sounds demanding and intimidating; the latter sounds more like simply an activity to engage in than an obligation to meet. It implies—and perhaps fosters—self-motivation. Understandably, Bell suggests listing duties in order of priority.

Toward the end of the job description, include the position's hours and pay. If salary is negotiable or commensurate with experience, say so. Give contact information for applying if the description is for a want ad as opposed to an internal document or record, plus a bit of background on your organization—a sentence or two about its history, focus, and philosophy or culture. Give the applicant a little taste of the big picture he or she will be a part of.

The sample job description included in *NTC's Business Writer's Handbook* mentions the dress code. I think that can be left to discuss in the interview. Common sense dictates that a new CFO will not show up for his or her first day on the job in a T-shirt and jeans, nor will a janitor or groundskeeper in a three-piece suit or (especially if he's a man) designer dress. Indeed, seeing what applicants will wear to the interview unprompted can help you gauge their seriousness.

Lastly, "Make job descriptions consistent within the company, using the same organizational pattern for each," recommends Bell. This strategy not only appears more professional, but can reinforce the company's priorities and expectations; consistently placing the same kind of information in the same order across all your descriptions conveys what aspects of the job your company considers more, and less, important. Writing informs both by what it says and by how it says it.

Many organizations use a standard form or protocol for employee performance reviews. If your format isn't pre-established—or if the pre-established format permits flexibility—here are some guidelines for writing reviews.

Diana Roberts Wienbroer et al. offer a technique for organizing descriptions of accomplishments, whether for personnel reviews or for company reports and publications, in *Rules of Thumb For Business Writers*. They suggest:

- Organize the accomplishments by type.
- Arrange the types in descending order of importance.
- Within each type, list accomplishments in chronological or hierarchical order.
- Find a unifying theme to use in the introduction and conclusion, and as transition between sections.

For thematic flow, you could instead group similar accomplishments and types of accomplishments together—for example, mention conducting training after mentioning giving presentations to clients, because both deal with personally imparting information to others. Finding a unifying theme per Wienbroer et al. also lends shape to the review: it provides a "thesis" for the review to "prove," a main idea that prevents the review from appearing like a collection of random facts about the person.

Be fair and, as Fox News would say, balanced in your performance review. If it consists entirely of praise without a single critical note, it would likely sound too good to be true (and probably would be), possibly arousing suspicions of favoritism in office superiors who would see your review. At the same time, keep criticism constructive, suggesting improvements to the employee's skills or working methods.

Also, take into account any mitigating factors. My former boss wrote in a performance review of me that when project managers come to us with work, I tend to be overprotective of our department's staff if we already have an enormous project or an urgent deadline, but then noted that this quality can have its virtues. It shows that I stick to priorities, avoid overextending resources, and don't like making unfulfillable promises. If I do say so myself.

Letters of recommendation can be organized like performance reviews—they're essentially performance reviews for an external audience. In *Rules of Thumb For Business Writers*, Wienbroer et al. arrange their sample letter of recommendation by a different pattern:

FIRST PARAGRAPH: Why you're writing.
SECOND PARAGRAPH: Background of your relationship with the subject and overview of the subject's duties.
THIRD PARAGRAPH: The subject's qualifications.
FOURTH PARAGRAPH: Conclusion. Offer further contact. If the subject is a current employee, explain why he or she is leaving.

Or you could approach the recommendation as a cover letter on the subject's behalf; the second paragraph could summarize his or her experience and skills, and the third paragraph could highlight his or her motivation for applying and how you think he or she would perform in the position.

I once worked for two months as an administrative assistant at an accounting firm. In the hopes of shortening the learning curve, the firm provided written instructions during my training for major tasks like processing clients' payroll. However, among the many irritations about the job that made my tenure so brief (by my decision, not theirs), I had to bug a co-worker or boss every few minutes because a step had been left out of the instructions and the computer program wouldn't let me proceed. Nothing if not forthright, I told the office manager once I had identified all the missing steps that the instructions were unclear and inadequate and should be revised—and that with my writing background I was just the man for the job. She agreed. My newness enabled me to write the instructions from the perspective of the people they were intended for: those who don't already know what they're doing.

You might think structuring instructions or directions shouldn't pose much of a challenge normally; just list each step in the order in which it must occur. But you should be mindful of a number of details in your instructions. Wienbroer et al. mention as one of the first things in their section on instructions and directions, "Define all unfamiliar terms." This especially applies to technical terms, and to names of parts in the case of product assembly instructions. You can't expect the customer to put the product together correctly without an explanation of things included in it that most consumers have never seen. As Angela Lunsford and Robert Connors, in *The New St. Martin's Handbook*, remark about writing in general,

> If you are writing an article for a journal for nurses about a drug that prevents patients from developing infections from intravenous feeding tubes, you will not need to give much information about how such tubes work or define many terms. But if you are writing about the same topic in a pamphlet for patients, you will have to give a great deal of background information and define (or avoid) technical terms.

"List the necessary materials and equipment," *Rules of Thumb For Business Writers* also states. A chef needs to know all of a dish's ingredients before cooking; that's why recipes list them first. Likewise, list all the parts included for the reader and name any unprovided tools or other materials the reader will need on hand (such as a screwdriver or glue) before starting with the steps of the procedure.

Wienbroer et al. note the most crucial element of writing instructions or directions from the novice's point of view: "Anticipate any possible misunderstandings.... Be careful not ... to assume that the reader will know something you haven't spelled out." This was the problem with the accounting firm's instructions—they assumed the little steps, taken for granted by those seasoned in performing the process, would also be taken for granted by beginners. They forgot what happens when you assume. In most cases you should beware of talking down to your reader, but the saying "explain this to me like I'm a five-year-old" epitomizes the best approach to writing instructions or directions.

In listing steps, strike a happy medium between conciseness and thoroughness. "*Don't* fragment instructions into an unmanageable number of little steps. Like parents assembling a complex toy on Christmas Eve, learners can feel overwhelmed by too many instructional cues," Bell warns. "*Don't* clutter straightforward directions with marginal asides, comments, and qualifications.... If your readers can do without an item of information, leave it out." While specialized terms or devices warrant definition and description, the audience does not need commentary or analysis on them. A work of writing should include only that which helps it achieve its purpose—whether presenting facts, arguing a position, or teaching someone how to do something. Rather, one can "find umbrella headings under which smaller steps and topics can find a place. Instead of a list of twenty small instructional steps for using a new word-processing system, seek out a few umbrella headings, with subtopics grouped beneath each umbrella," advises Bell. Include everything you legitimately need, but streamline the instructions' format on the page to lessen the apparent weight of information, arranging them into convenient groups of related actions.

For more complex procedures, *NTC's Business Writer's Handbook* recommends touching on the following issues:

1. An Overview. Begin the process explanation by conveying the 'big picture.' What is the process called? What in the experience of the audience could it be compared to?
2. Division of Parts. What are the distinct parts of the process? What are those parts called? Why?
3. Interrelation of Parts. How do individual parts relate? Which are most important to your discussion?
4. Outcomes of the Process. What does the process produce? What helps or hinders that production?
5. Evaluation. What works well or poorly in the process? What changes are recommended?

One difficulty with this approach (and with writing instructions in general) is that the writer usually doesn't know much about the audience. Procedure instructions' audience consists of new employees whose experience and expectations you've as yet learned only the bare outline of, and for product assembly or operation directions the audience is a mass of people you'll never meet. Therefore, your writing must be as transparent and broadly accessible as possible.

Describing the interrelation of parts could be beneficial when one has to temporarily stop working on one component and switch to another component; the reader will avoid feeling lost if he or she understands while reading the directions why he or she must go back and forth between parts. In this way, too, instructions should be like recipes: we don't mind suspending our work on the meat to work on the sauce because we know they both need to be attended to differently at different stages of the preparation, and know the role each will play once they are combined.

Concerning results, Wienbroer et al. instruct, "Describe how the product will look at each stage or how the worker will know the step is successful ..." Providing signposts throughout the process—not just at the end—to show the reader whether he or she is following it correctly is another important way to prevent him or her from feeling lost.

An evaluation is seldom necessary. Your procedure should be the best possible for your task, unless management imposed it or you inherited it from predecessors and you lack the authority to change it. Then you might want to add a note about difficulties and any ways one could avoid or circumvent them. Otherwise, don't write about the instructions' problems—solve them.

Instructions resemble other forms of writing in the part style plays in their readability. Instructions—as the most information-driven, nuts-and-bolts kind of business writing—lend themselves to short, pithy sentences. *Rules of Thumb For Business Writers* observes, "The simple sentence is the most common kind of sentence in modern English, but using only simple sentences can sound very dull. On the other hand, overusing compound sentences may result in a singsong or repetitive rhythm, and strings of complex sentences may sound, well, overly complex." Instructions are inherently dry. We only read them when and because we have to, and their purpose precludes much in their content from enlivening them; they are purely utilitarian writing. Thus, you should rely on style to keep the reader engaged, and variation of sentence structure serves as the main weapon in your arsenal. Lunsford and Connors elaborate, "Row upon row of trees identical in size and shape may appeal at some level to a sense of orderliness, but those identical rows soon become boring. If variety is the spice of life, it is also the spice of sentence structure, whereas sameness can result in dull, listless prose."

Human beings are curious by nature, and headstrong. We like to know why things are the way they are, and we get dissatisfied when we feel that things are not as they should be. Therefore, Wienbroer et al. recommend, "Explain why you suggest doing a step a certain way....

> To protect your hands and to ensure sanitation, wear clean, heavy-duty rubber gloves while securing the jar lids."

Their advice especially relates to procedure directions at work. The worker will feel more invested in the task, will feel it's more worthwhile, if he or she understands the rationale of the directions as given. Employees bucking the system because task directions *appear* inefficient or counterintuitive can lead to poor work as well as to low morale—they'll think higher-ups are out of touch with the company's real operation.

For the final step in foolproofing your instructions, *Rules of Thumb For Business Writers* prescribes, "With your instructions in hand, follow each and every step.... Then ask a colleague unfamiliar with the process to follow the instructions." Auto manufacturers run their cars through road and crash tests to ensure their operability and safety before deeming them market-worthy. Similarly, you should test how well your instructions fulfill their function before releasing them for use, even if they concern a less potentially dangerous process than driving. The consequences of skipping this step may not cost lives, but could cost your livelihood and credibility.

EXPOSITORY BUSINESS WRITING

Expository writing mainly relates information to the reader. It can take many forms: newspaper articles, restaurant menus, legal briefs, laboratory reports, encyclopedias. It makes up the bulk of professional writing—it's a major way in which businesses keep tabs on themselves. But expository writing entails more than just throwing facts onto paper. The writer must establish the credibility of his or her information in the eyes of the reader, and at times must interpret it; he or she must provide a sound foundation for his or her findings.

The most prevalent and most important type of expository writing in the business world is the annual report, in which a business summarizes its operations and their results for the foregoing fiscal year. In *NTC's Business Writer's Handbook*, Arthur H. Bell describes the annual report's purpose as "to build goodwill among shareholders and to sell its image as a successful company to others." It aims to keep current investors happy and attract new ones. The report should also state the company's "long- and short-term objectives."

The annual report begins with an introduction abstracting the report's content. "The introduction features a letter of transmittal, usually from the president or chairman of the board," writes Bell. "This brief letter ... highlights the year's activities and attempts to communicate strength, confidence, and stability."

Bell notes that annual reports usually consist of a narrative section and a financial section. The narrative section concerns the business writer. The financial section consists mostly of raw numbers; leave that for the CFO and the accountants. *NTC's Business Writer's Handbook* enumerates ten areas the narrative section of the annual report should include.

Products and Services—Self-explanatory, although Bell adds, "Future markets, advertising and marketing programs are usually treated here."

Plants and Equipment—Discusses the physical apparatus of the business: land, buildings, machinery, vehicles, and so forth. The *Handbook* comments, "In addition, information on projected capital costs and return on investments"—what the company expects to spend in this area and whether new property or equipment has been or will be worth the expense—"often is presented." Bell mentions "expansion of facilities" as a topic of particular importance in the annual report; that would most likely fall under this heading.

Employees—This section deals with the size of the workforce, payroll, affirmative action, other human resources concerns, and outstanding individual achievements.

Labor Relations—On a related note, this section treats labor relations and union activity such as collective bargaining or strikes—"as objectively as possible," Bell highlights.

Stockholders—Discusses issues regarding the company's stock and investors, including "the number of stockholders, the distribution of their holdings, and their interest in the company."

Government Relations—The annual report should devote a section to the firm's "relations with government and regulatory agencies.... legislation that might impact the company and the interests of federal agencies are addressed as well." Furthermore, presumably for government contractors, note the "percentage of the firm's production that goes to the government."

Community Relations—Does your company participate in the Walk for Hunger, Walk for a Cure, or Adopt-A-Highway program? Does it sponsor community activities or charities or encourage employees to volunteer? Put that in a part on community relations.

Research and Development—Another key area. *NTC's Business Writer's Handbook* states, "Without giving away company secrets, new developments or trends may be discussed briefly. Further, the portion of company profits reinvested in research and development work may be disclosed."

Social Issues—Some corporations might have a significant stake in social and political issues in public debate. Lumber or oil companies might hold a particular philosophy about conservation, and insurance and pharmaceutical companies might concern themselves with discussion of universal health care. Mention in your annual report if your company takes a stand on any social issues, what that stand is, and what if anything (lobbying, sponsoring public service messages, or the like) the company does to influence opinion or policy on those issues.

Legal Issues—In this section, discuss any legal proceedings the company is involved in—especially lawsuits against the company—and the likely financial impact they will have.

To me, it makes more sense to arrange these sections differently. Research and Development seems like the most important subject after Products and Services; the former leads to the latter. The third section would be Stockholders: they are, after all, the primary audience for the annual report, and the most basic thing to know about a company after what it does is who owns it and where it gets its capital. After reviewing the company's financial wherewithal, proceed to its material wherewithal in Plants and Equipment, and its human wherewithal in Employees and Labor Relations could follow. Next I would place Government Relations and Legal Issues, because of the remaining sections they relate most directly to the operation of the business. I'd end the report with the more ancillary aspects of the business, Social Issues and Community Relations.

Data reports also often play a vital role in business, whether they report findings from a laboratory test, results of a product trial (like crash tests for cars), or responses from a survey of consumers. All data reports should contain a section describing the methodology of the test or survey. "Limitations of the investigation should be noted," comments Bell, "....The research methods used should be explained as well as how validity or reliability of the survey was secured." You want to convince your audience that the findings of the experiment, trial, or survey indeed resulted from the factors attributed, and not from the interference of outside factors that the test failed to consider and control for or from chance. Thus, for laboratory tests or product trials discuss materials and instruments used, how conditions for the experiment were created, and the use of comparison subjects; for surveys note criteria for participation, techniques for randomizing the sample or making it demographically representative, and statistical methods used.

Summarize the results in an abstract, introduction, or executive summary. The body of a laboratory report will resemble that of an article in a scientific journal. Provide background into the nature of the experiment's topic and any previous research on it. State your hypothesis and explain the reasoning behind it. Describe the experiment's methodology, relate the data resulting from the test in depth, and present a conclusion based on the data. Structure a product trial report similarly, but begin with the methodology because your audience already knows the purpose and background of the trial. A survey report starts with methodology and an executive summary, then is divided into sections based on the type of questions asked, with the most fundamental and/or important information treated first. Often results are overviewed and, if applicable, analyzed only in the executive summary at the beginning of the report, not in a concluding section, so the reader can learn the upshot of the study immediately. Rather, an appendix will contain demographic data on participants.

An activity report briefly reviews a company's activity of a certain type within a certain time period. *NTC's Business Writer's Handbook* provides the following model for structuring an activity report:

> "Sales of Franchises in the Third Quarter"
> I.   Overview
>   Purpose of this report, time period covered, geographical area covered, summary of sales from past quarter.
> II. Third Quarter Results
>   Statistical summary of sales—who sold what to whom, where, when, and perhaps why.
> III. Interpretation of Sales Results
>   What we learned from third quarter sales: techniques that worked and didn't work; star performers and snails; analysis of strong areas and weak areas.
> IV. Conclusions, with a Recommendation
>   Summary statement of third quarter results, with appropriate recommendation for emphasizing strong points and minimizing weak points.

When developing the information in your writing chronologically, as in the activity report, Bell offers this advice: "Make time divisions appropriate for your argument. Don't skip over large blocks of time when your purpose requires a close examination of individual days, weeks, or months. At the same time, don't trivialize a broad, general argument by taking unnecessarily small steps through the time span you've chosen." Maintain a sense of scope. On a world map, the key gives the distance measured in miles, whereas a floor plan measures distance only in feet. Similarly, the narrative section of an annual report would view events month by month or quarter by quarter. The *Handbook*'s model activity report, however, with a scope limited to one quarter, would treat events more minutely, by weeks or perhaps by months.

Progress reports differ from activity reports in that they deal with single projects rather than entire classes of projects, and because they chart the lifespan of a project, whatever that may be, not a set unit of time like a business quarter. As the name implies, organizing by chronological development best suits progress reports. Bell writes, "Most managers prefer progress reports that provide a brief background to the situation, a detailed summary of the period covered, and a statement of the work to be carried through during the next time block. Problems and obstacles encountered are usually noted in detail with recommendations for solutions."

When something untoward or unwelcome occurs at work, management will often call for a trouble report to review the incident. The sample trouble report in *NTC's Business Writer's Handbook* opens by noting when and how the problem was first reported. Continue with how the problem evolved. Then describe the company's investigation into the problem, its findings, and any action taken by the company—as well as the likely consequences of such action on the parties involved and the company. "Be specific and descriptive about causes, effects, parts, processes, personnel and other aspects of the problem," counsels Bell. And as with describing labor relations in the annual report, "Be objective. Report facts about what happened, not speculations on the motives or abilities of others (unless you are asked to do so)."

For the gravest problems, the company might order a report concentrating more minutely on the investigation itself. Bell gives a plan for the investigative report that consists of a description of the problem, a description of the investigation's methodology (a narrative of the investigation's process could be woven in here or serve as a separate section), a discussion of the investigation's findings, and a conclusion with recommendations. Bell qualifies this last point, though: "The investigator in many cases is not asked to make recommendations, which may more properly be left to higher levels of review within the company." Treating methodology is important in the interest of transparency: it will assure those affected by the investigation's outcome that the company obtained the information used in making its decisions fairly. As the methodology section in a data report demonstrates that the study covered all its scientific bases, in an investigative report it establishes the investigation's ethical validity.

Take care with the extent of your interpretation when an expository report calls for it. Make sure your interpretation is firmly rooted in and refers back to the facts presented earlier, the essence of expository writing, and keep the amount of space devoted to interpretation substantially less than that devoted to presenting information. Too much analysis or opinion in an expository report can cause it to spill over into persuasive writing when the occasion doesn't call for it.

§

How does a writer establish the factuality of information for the reader? Aristotle considered this question in his *Rhetoric,* the classic textbook for expository and persuasive writing. He called the literary techniques used for expository writing "forensic rhetoric," because—like forensics in a criminal investigation—they establish fact.

The most basic way is to cite an authoritative source for the information. If you need to state that a certain number of surveys came in or that a specific survey was received on a certain date, mention that you obtained this information from a daily tracker of incoming surveys to assure the reader that you're relying on timely records of such details and not on fuzzy human memory or guesstimation. If you need to state the quantity of a specific product manufactured, refer to a production log or readings of instruments that count units processed. When discussing shipping, cite pack lists or cargo manifests. Financial data might come from receipts, invoices, ledger or journal entries, or figures entered into financial software programs like Sage or QuickBooks. Other valid sources include legal documents such as contracts, correspondence, and testimony from people you've interviewed. Interviewees should have a direct connection to the subject of your report: they should have worked on the project it focuses on or have witnessed events it discusses.

But first-hand sources are not the only way of determining factuality—fortunately, because they're not always available. One can demonstrate the factuality of a premise based on the already accepted, or obvious, truth of other related facts. This method is commonly called by its philosophical name, the syllogism; it is also called, according to Aristotle, by the rhetorical term the enthymeme. The most widely known example of the syllogism, found in many primers on logic, goes like this: All men are mortal; Socrates is a man; therefore Socrates is mortal. While Socrates remains alive, we have no empirical, primary proof of his mortality, but we may combine the two preceding already known facts to establish it as fact.

To employ syllogisms effectively, the two supporting facts should be expressed separately and share one concept in common, as the idea of "man" is held in common by the major, more universal premise "All men are mortal" and by the minor, more particular, premise "Socrates is a man." The shared idea should bracket or sandwich the two statements of fact.

However, "…if one were to say that all wise men are just, because Socrates was both wise and just…. even though the particular statement is true, it can be refuted, because it cannot be reduced to syllogistic form," Aristotle explains. First, the claim contains two common concepts, wisdom and justice—one too many for a logically cohesive syllogism. Moreover, both qualities simultaneously are ascribed to Socrates and then justice is immediately extended to all wise men, without demonstrating either justice's dependence on wisdom or Socrates' commonality with all wise men. A fact can be proven by other facts only when it results from combining two other statements of fact, not from the mere coincidence of two qualities or conditions.

Certain categories of facts, which Aristotle calls "topics," lend themselves most readily to forensic rhetoric. Aristotle alluded to one of the most important above: causation. This "topic consists in concluding the identity of antecedents from the identity of results," he says—in other words, the nature of present conditions derive from the nature of past conditions. The *Rhetoric* offers this example: "…it is a sign that a man is ill, because he has a fever, or that a woman has had a child because she has milk…" If we add statements of the familiar facts that all fevers result from illness and that all lactation results from recent pregnancy, we can create syllogisms proving that the illness produced the fever, that the pregnancy produced the milk.

Bell warns us, however, about common fallacies committed when trying to prove cause. First, not everything that follows something is caused by it; or, seen from a different perspective, the cause of an event or condition isn't always its most obvious antecedent. The true cause may slip subtly under our radars. Many who suffer from late summer allergies believe they are triggered by the goldenrod sprouting through cracks in sidewalks everywhere and bending under its load of yellow flowers that bloom days before they start sniffling and sneezing. The real culprit is ragweed, which, because much less conspicuous, many people don't take account of. Also, "a cause is not the *only* cause," Bell writes. Lastly, "Causal links are not necessarily predictive of the future. Just because Situation A caused Situation B at one time does not mean it will always produce the same result."

Another widely used topic mentioned by Aristotle is "the possible and the impossible." We can turn Aristotle's examples above on their heads and prove that a man cannot possibly have a fever because he is not ill, since fever can only possibly occur as a result of illness; and that a woman cannot be lactating because she has not had a baby recently, since it is impossible for a woman to lactate without having given birth recently.

When interpreting findings in expository reports, writers most often use inductive logic, which "reaches its statement of major truths only after compiling a series of minor truths." Inductive logic moves from the specific to the general; it arrives at an overall conclusion by considering each individual fact. In many cases, these individual facts fall into a category that the conclusion identifies. Aristotle in the *Rhetoric* observes, "There is an instance of this in the

Socrates of Theodectes: 'What holy place has he profaned? Which of the gods recognized by the city has he neglected to honor?'" Socrates was accused by the city of Athens of impiety. The speaker defends him against this charge by identifying aspects of impiety and showing that Socrates has not committed any of them. The previous examples of fever and lactation from Aristotle operate by category as well as by causation: fever falls into the category of symptoms of illness, and lactation falls into the category of the aftermath of pregnancy.

Like causation, though, argument by classification lends itself to certain fallacies. Aristotle elaborates, "…for instance, if one were to say that this man has a fever, because he breathes hard; but even if the fact be true, this argument can also be refuted, for it is possible for a man to breathe hard without having a fever." Heavy breathing does fall under the category of symptoms of fever, but does not fall exclusively under that category; it can just as likely be a sign of emphysema, suffocation, exhaustion, or making an obscene phone call. Argument by classification convinces most forcefully when the specifics are unique to the category they are ascribed to—what Aristotle calls "necessary signs." Also similarly to causation, don't confuse a coincident relationship with one between a category and its particulars. The *Rhetoric*'s case of arguing that all wise men are just because Socrates was both wise and just fails, in part, because it doesn't establish justice as a subset of wisdom.

We see then that even expository writing is a form of argument: although we don't argue for the validity of our opinions as in persuasive writing, we must argue, implicitly or explicitly, our information's factuality and on occasion establish its significance. As it happens, Aristotle modeled his analysis of forensic rhetoric on the legal case, in which the attorneys must use the several particular facts of the case to lead the jury to the larger conclusion of the defendant's guilt or innocence. Forensic rhetoric requires a logical rigor that binds us to the facts we present, leaving little room for speculation or conjecture. If we can adhere to this rigor successfully, we'll have a rhetorical leg up in persuasive writing for using fact in a secondary capacity to bolster our opinions.

PERSUASIVE BUSINESS WRITING

More rides on persuasive writing than on any other kind of writing in business. Persuasive writing influences organizations to make important decisions and undertake major initiatives; a poor argument for a good idea could lead a company to make the worst mistake of its existence. In the boardroom as in the courtroom, convincing your audience depends as much on how you present your case as it does on the facts and circumstances that indicate its rightness. You have to show the audience why those facts and circumstances make your case right.

This chapter will focus on the proposal, the form of persuasive writing most common in professional settings. It will give you the essentials of organization, argument, and style for the most crucial type of writing you might ever need to practice at the office.

§

An effective proposal consists of four parts. My Advanced Composition class in college spent most of the semester producing a proposal. We concentrated on one part at a time, each building upon and added onto the last, until we finally had a complete proposal at course's end— just as a house might be built floor by floor. I think this model of writing in stages helps the writer deal with the various sections of the proposal, each with its different content and demands.

The first part of the proposal is called the categorical proposition, a term from logic that means you demonstrate that the situation your proposal seeks to remedy exists. If you are proposing a new product for your company, your categorical proposition would prove the need for this product and that a market exists that your company has left untapped. In my Advanced Composition class I proposed increasing Metrobus (the D.C. area's public bus system) service through the University of Maryland campus. I first established the limited extent of public transportation to and from campus: only one Metrobus route ran through campus, which didn't go to Prince George's Plaza, the closest major shopping mall and a favorite student destination; and the university's shuttle bus service ended shortly after 7:00 p.m. and did not run on weekends.

Arthur H. Bell explains in *NTC's Business Writer's Handbook,*

Any document or oral presentation claiming to analyze or make recommendations regarding a problem must first state the problem clearly and concisely. This statement should answer the following questions:

What is the problem?
Where is it occurring?
When is it occurring?
How is it occurring?
To whom is it occurring?
Why is it occurring?

(This last question, because of its breadth, may be reserved for later portions of the analysis.)

The problem statement appears early in a document or oral presentation to orient the audience to the topic under discussion.

Don't inject your opinion about the situation into the categorical proposition; keep its content factual. Proving the situation exists will rely on citing authoritative sources for your information. For my bus proposal I cited Metro and shuttle bus schedules, and interviews with Metro and shuttle bus staff and with students and university employees who frequently took public transportation. Good sources for your proposals might include other company reports and documents, market or opinion research data, government census or demographic data, books on your topic, or trade journal articles.

In the second part of the proposal, argue that the situation described in the categorical proposition is a problem. Evaluation of the situation comes in here: describe the negative consequences the situation has on your audience and possibly on others. *NTC's Business Writer's Handbook* lists questions a writer can ask himself or herself and answer in a problem analysis to flesh it out:

"1. What name can be given to the problem?" The name can be very simple, like "insufficient bus service." Sometimes a single word or phrase won't capture the nature of the problem adequately, though. It should have a negative connotation to reinforce its problem status.

"2. How can the problem be described?" What exactly makes it a problem? If you pitched a new product idea to your company, the problem would be that by not producing such an item your company fails to capitalize on sales opportunities and stunts its market share and visibility, while leaving its customers—both current and potential—with an unfulfilled need. (As much as possible, use hard numbers to support your description.)

"3. What are its parts?" A complex problem may contain a number of aspects, each of which requires attention. The problem of Metrobus service to the University of Maryland consisted of several problems within it. On-campus students had inconvenient access to one of their favorite shopping locations: a university shuttle bus went to Prince George's Plaza, but not on weekends when students had the most free time. Many students living off-campus couldn't get to campus on weekends—say, to research in the library—or stay late on campus for events like movies, plays, concerts, readings, or lectures or to participate in campus organizations' activities. Employees not living near the campus's existing Metrobus route or a university shuttle bus route and who relied on public transportation had a difficult commute, often entailing multiple bus transfers.

You may find that the problem extends farther than you had initially thought. I realized that the lack of sufficient bus service from campus hurt local merchants like those at Prince George's Plaza, costing them business from students quite eager to shop, although I hadn't thought of them when I decided to write the proposal.

"4. What are its causes?" Your proposal should strike the problem at its roots; identify those roots.

"5. What are its effects?" An effect of the problem in our hypothetical product proposal might be customer dissatisfaction. Effects of insufficient Metrobus service in my Advanced Composition proposal included a sense of isolation from the local community among students living on campus, a sense of exclusion from campus life among off-campus students relying on public transportation, and low morale among campus workers who also depended on public transportation.

"6. What is its history?" Relate how the causes led to the problem and its effects, and whether the problem and effects have remained constant over time or have evolved.

"7. What can it be compared to?" Does the problem resemble anything else in the audience's experience or that you could expect your audience to be familiar with?

"8. What feelings are aroused by it?" You could, of course, address this under Questions 2 and 5.

The proposal's third section explains the benefits of solving the problem—usually, simply the reversal of its problematic aspects for all involved. The benefits of our hypothetical proposal to the company would be increased revenue and market share, higher customer satisfaction, and, if venturing into a new sector, diversification or comprehensiveness of its product line. Customers would benefit by having their demands supplied by quality goods, ideally for an affordable price and at convenient locations. And just as a problem often extends beyond its immediate scope, its resolution will benefit people other than those primarily intended. Employees would benefit from the availability of more work; depending on the scale of production, the local economy where the company will manufacture the product might benefit from the creation of new jobs (which could in turn generate community goodwill for the company). The company would give more business to its vendors and suppliers, deepening existing relationships or forging strategic new ones. Retailers selling the product will have one more item to bring people through the doors.

In my bus proposal, most of the direct benefits of expanding Metrobus service to campus would accrue to parties other than my audience, Metro. Students could more easily travel to their most needed and desired local destinations and commuter students would be able to get to and from campus at night and on weekends. This would enable on-campus students to feel more connected to the area rather than sequestered on an academic island and commuter students to feel they can play a part in university life, contributing to a positive view of their student experience overall. High student satisfaction means the University of Maryland could attract prospective new students competitively. University employees would benefit from a smoother commute to work and back, raising their morale—which, similarly to the case of students, would make the university attractive to applicants for open positions. The area's economy would benefit because students, and maybe employees, would have access to more local goods and services. Nonetheless, I emphasized that all of the above would ultimately benefit Metro through increased fare revenue, as well as the intangible assets of rider satisfaction and goodwill.

Last comes your actual proposal, your suggestion for solving the problem. "Describe in detail your proposed plan of attack," Bell advises.

Are your methods proven?... What personnel will be involved? What is their training? What time schedule have you established for your work? What are the major checkpoints in that schedule?

Also discuss your plan of evaluation. What significant indications of progress will you look for? When? How will you measure success? Will your research results be observable? Preservable? Repeatable?

Not every question will apply to every proposal, but this list represents a good outline for ensuring your proposal's thoroughness. The more you can ground your proposal in operational detail, the better you can convince your audience of its viability: it means you really know what it takes to get the job done, that you can walk the walk as well as talk the talk.

When proposing a new product to your company, you'd want to include plans for the design of the product; the materials, equipment, and amount of labor needed to manufacture it; a production schedule; how the product will be distributed; and who will retail it. My proposal for Metrobus service to the University of Maryland was a bit simpler, since it didn't involve a series of processes like the product proposal example. I proposed changing another bus route that started in the blue-collar area near the D.C. line where many university employees lived, ran up U.S. Route 1 alongside campus, and continued past it. I re-routed it to turn onto Campus Drive, the university's main drag, and then make its way through the local roads to Prince George's Plaza.

Your proposal should demonstrate knowledge of the operational and logistical requirements to enact what you propose, and of the resources at your audience's disposal to enact it. In the *Rhetoric*, Aristotle asks rhetorically (appropriately enough): "I should like to know, for instance, how we are to give advice to the Athenians as to making war or not, if we do not know in what their strength consists, whether it is naval, military, or both, how great it is, their sources of revenue, their friends and enemies, and further, what wars they have already waged, with what success, and all similar things?" I knew that Metro might be experiencing growing pains, having opened the subway's Green Line only a year and a half before, which could make it wary of extending its capabilities too much and too quickly. I also learned from a newspaper article that Metro's bus drivers were among the highest-paid in the nation—any increase in bus service could have carried with it a large continuous price tag in payroll. Therefore my proposal minimized the change to Metro's *status quo*.

After outlining your proposal, show explicitly how it solves the problem and benefits those affected—how it removes the conditions described in the problem section and how it provides the advantages you said solving the problem would bring. I pointed out that my re-routing idea gave students direct bus access between campus and Prince George's Plaza and gave commuter students in a larger part of Prince George's County convenient Metrobus service to campus, including greater weekend service. The large number of employees living south of College Park would have an easier bus commute to work. Metro would gain extra fare revenue in addition to customer satisfaction and goodwill. Moreover, the university would gain goodwill from its students and employees, and the local economy would get a little boost.

Also note any unique advantages to your proposal that you didn't mention in the third section. I made sure to indicate that re-routing an existing bus line would not cause Metro to overextend itself. They didn't need to commit any additional vehicles or new staff to realize the plan, making their expenditure of money, equipment, and personnel for it virtually nil.

Thorough awareness of your proposal's advantages can help with the final important part of presenting it: refuting possible objections. Your audience may receive other proposals advocating different plans, or may resist or doubt the effectiveness of elements of your own plan. If you can knock down the most likely rival ideas and obstacles in your audience's perception to implementing your own, the stronger yours will stand out to your audience as a result.

Nothing in this world is perfect. Any proposal will have some kind of flaw or drawback, something less than ideal; if you acknowledge this disadvantage but can diminish its significance, the reader will see that you have thought your proposal out carefully and have a full grasp of it, and that therefore it is worth seriously considering. In many decisions, all the possible options have both compelling positives and compelling negatives. Aristotle describes such a situation in the *Rhetoric*: "For instance, education is attended by the evil of being envied, and by the good of being wise; therefore we should not be educated, for we should avoid being envied; nay rather, we *should* be educated, for we should be wise." Aim to persuade the reader that the advantages of your proposal outweigh any disadvantages. You could also argue that the disadvantages are less severe than they initially appear or are even illusory.

Consider whether alternatives exist or could arise, and think about ways to prove your proposal's superiority to them. I knew the most likely other option to my Metrobus proposal would be for the university shuttle bus service or the Prince George's County public transportation service, distinctively named "The Bus," to provide the route. I argued that the University of Maryland's business is education, not transportation; as a state school supported largely by public funds, one could expect it to spare little of its resources to grow a service as loosely tied to its mission as bus service, especially as it campaigned to increase its scholarly prestige. Proponents of The Bus administering the increased service to campus could point to Ride On, the local bus system of Montgomery County, Prince George's neighbor to the west, as a model for local jurisdictions meeting their citizens' public transportation needs in tandem with Metro. However, I wrote, Montgomery County's inhabitants were generally more affluent than Prince George's County's. Its local government received more tax money from them and could fund a much more robust (the most annoyingly overused business-parlance word of the 21st Century) bus system. Since The Bus operated on such a small scale that I had never seen it before and hadn't known it existed until I researched this proposal, I argued the implausibility of Prince George's County affording to add a major route to it.

The end of your proposal should look ahead to working with your audience to implement your plan. "Conclude your proposal by expressing your willingness to answer questions and provide further information...perhaps to consider reshaping your proposal as necessary to meet the needs of the client or agency," Bell writes. He also states that in terms of evaluating the results of their proposals, "Often, proposal writers describe their ultimate goals as a series of achievement plateaus, any one of which justifies the work proposed. In this way, writers allow funding agencies to feel that even if the highest predictions of their proposals bear no fruit, important results can nonetheless be accomplished at plateaus along the way." Just as nothing in this world is perfect, we can't always get what we want—as the Rolling Stones tell us—and what we get often doesn't come out the way we intended. Remember, and convey to your reader, that realizing even a part of your plan would be a victory.

§

Aristotle calls the kind of rhetoric used in persuasive writing or oratory "deliberative rhetoric": it involves deciding whether or not to do something. He identifies three components of deliberative rhetoric—logos, ethos, and pathos—and observes that "every speech is composed of three parts: the speaker, the subject of which he treats, and the person to whom it is addressed..." Rhetoricians over the ages have associated each of deliberative rhetoric's components with a party in the rhetorical situation to produce a model called the "rhetorical triangle" that can guide you to meet the basic requirements of any persuasive writing situation. Logos, the logic of the argument, focuses on the writing's subject. Ethos deals with the writer's character as conveyed in his or her writing. Pathos is the emotional element of the argument, concentrating on the audience's instinctive reaction to the argument.

Logos is the most important part of any argument, standing at the top of the rhetorical triangle; if your argument's line of reasoning doesn't hold up, your readers will dismiss it out of hand. Deductive logic, which shows general principles to be the cause of specific items, proves most apt for persuasive writing. Deductive logic, even more than inductive logic as treated in the previous chapter, frequently uses the syllogism to structure its arguments. I could apply the syllogism model to the proposal for increasing local bus service through the University of Maryland campus. The major premise would state the overarching problem: "Metrobus service to the University of Maryland is inadequate." The minor premise would delineate the specific nature of the problem, for example, "On-campus students dependent on public transportation have no way to get to Prince George's Plaza on weekends." This leads to the conclusion "A Metrobus route should run through campus to Prince George's Plaza." For multifaceted proposals like mine, you can plug other aspects of the problem—like the needs of off-campus students and of employees—into the syllogism as other minor premises. Your plan would then need to incorporate the results of each syllogism.

Sometimes one of the premises of a syllogism is so universally familiar that stating it outright would just waste words. As Aristotle's *Rhetoric* comments, "For instance, to prove that Dorieus was the victor in a contest at which the prize was a crown, it is enough to say that he won a victory at the Olympic games; there is no need to add that the prize at the Olympic games is a crown, for everybody knows it." You wouldn't have to "prove" that the United States became independent in 1776 by mentioning that the Declaration of Independence was signed in that year.

NTC's Business Writer's Handbook's following example of the syllogism's use in deduction describes a complication relevant to writing proposals:

> All competing blood pressure monitors are inaccurate.
> Brand X is a competing blood pressure monitor.
> Therefore, Brand X is inaccurate.

Bell continues, "You may be feeling what the client may feel: 'Wait a minute. The VP is relying too much on the truth of the initial assertion. How does the VP know that all competing blood pressure monitors are inaccurate?'... You sense that the 'truth,' if it is to be stated in a more compelling way, must be supported by another form of logic." That form is induction, which establishes general principles by examining specific ones—the opposite of deduction. Proposals argue about single particular situations. Where, then, do their general premises come from? This is why the first half of a proposal demonstrates the situation's existence and its status as a problem; the proposal I wrote in college for increasing bus service to the University of Maryland could only explain the benefits of doing so and how my plan would bring those benefits by proving beforehand that current service was insufficient. The assembling of specific facts about the problem in the earlier, more expository part of the proposal produces the general principles that we argue from in the persuasive part.

Many other rhetorical devices can support the syllogism in proving an argument in persuasive writing. Among the best is citing authorities on your subject; the top minds in the field agreeing with your opinion can only give it more weight. Rhetoricians cited authority for support as early as Aristotle: "Witnesses are of two kinds, ancient and recent ... By ancient I mean the poets and men of repute whose judgments are known to all; for instance, the Athenians, in the matter of Salamis, appealed to Homer as a witness …" "Ancient witnesses" in the *Rhetoric* clearly equals what we mean by "authority": a well-known source whose insight into a certain subject is generally regarded as wise. Aristotle adds, "One should appeal to such witnesses for the past, but also to interpreters of oracles for the future …" Experts can predict or speculate on future trends or courses of events in addition to interpreting past phenomena. In place of the supposedly supernatural revelations of ancient oracles, today we have the analysis of those who in the world of political commentary—and they have their counterparts in business writing—go by the term "pundit."

Another device works like, and is basically a special type of, citing authority. "If," write Angela Lunsford and Robert Connors in *The New St. Martin's Handbook*, "as part of a proposal for increased lighting in the library garage, you point out that the university has increased lighting in four similar garages in the past year, you are arguing on the basis of precedent." Arguing by precedent can function in two ways. By comparing present circumstances to past, we indicate that we should treat those circumstances the same way they were treated before—or that we should learn from our previous mistakes. "It would be an instance of the historical kind of example," Aristotle explains,

> if one were to say that it is necessary to make preparations against the Great King and not allow him to subdue Egypt; for Darius did not cross over to Greece until he had obtained possession of Egypt; but as soon as he had done so, he did. Again, Xerxes did not attack us until he had obtained possession of that country, but when he had, he crossed over; consequently, if the present Great King should do the same, he will cross over, wherefore it must not be allowed.

It also appeals to consistency, as when used in legal arguments. An argument employing precedent demands that the audience act in the present according to the same principles that guided it in similar past situations to avoid the appearance of a double-standard or of arbitrariness.

Analogy offers one of the most vivid and succinct rhetorical supports. Bell comments, "Analogies are useful … to help express difficult, unfamiliar, or uninteresting ideas." More than explaining, the thing compared to symbolizes the thing compared, making explanation all but unnecessary or else summarizing or encapsulating explanation. We writers always scold one another, "Show, don't tell"—well, think of analogy when you don't know how to show or tell. Analogy furthermore widens the scope of the argument by comparing your topic to something outside of itself. The other frame of reference can reveal qualities of the situation otherwise lost on an audience attending to the situation short-sightedly on its own terms, as in Lunsford and Connors's example: "A student arguing for a more streamlined course registration process may find good use for an analogy, saying that the current registration process makes students feel like laboratory rats in a maze." Analogy can also highlight weaknesses or inconsistencies in an opposing argument; the *Rhetoric* relates, "… Iphicrates, when they tried to force his son to perform public services because he was tall, although under the legal age, said: 'If you consider tall boys men, you must vote that short men are boys.'"

Relating a specific incident concerning the problem illustrates to your audience the nature and extent of the problem's impact; hence, anecdotes help powerfully in persuasion. Moreover, *NTC's Business Writer's Handbook* mentions, "Anecdotes offer the audience a refreshing distraction from a complex or lengthy discussion. They help to establish rapport between the speaker and the audience and serve to humanize the speaker's message." At the same time, remember that your audience won't read your proposal for entertainment. Keep your persuasive writing just that—persuasive. (I'd argue that *interlude* would have been a better word for Bell to choose than "distraction.") *The New St. Martin's Handbook* cautions, "If you use stories in an argument, make sure they are used not merely to add interest but rather to support your thesis."

I included an anecdote about a University of Maryland custodian named Bennie Pender's daily commute to campus in my proposal on Metrobus service. Bennie lived in Brentwood, a town bordering Washington. From home he took the bus I wanted to re-route heading north on U.S. Route 1 to College Park. On the edge of campus, he had to get off that bus and cross the highway to catch the bus that passed through campus in order to get to the building where he worked on the other side of campus. Bennie had to pay for both buses: he couldn't transfer because the buses ran along Route 1 in opposite directions. His story illustrated how the inefficiency of Metrobus service to the university complicated its passengers' daily lives.

Apart from helping prove ideas, anecdotes can also punctuate them, encapsulate them for emphasis in the way analogy does. The president of Yeshiva University, Richard Joel, once spoke at a synagogue I attend. He talked about the college's philosophy of combining religious and secular education, and told a story about the father of a prospective student who felt that philosophy ineffective. He challenged Joel: "Will the next *godol ha-dor* [great Torah scholar of the generation] come from YU or from Lakewood"—an overwhelmingly Orthodox community and center of Jewish learning in New Jersey. "Will the next Nobel laureate come from YU or from Yale?" Joel said he replied, "I don't know. But I do know that the next Nobel laureate will not come from Lakewood, and the next *godol ha-dor* will not come from Yale. They both *might* come from YU." That story made Joel's point better than any abstract discussion of philosophical or doctrinal principles ever could.

One can even use plausible hypothetical anecdotes, provided one discloses that they are imaginary. "Fables are suitable for public speaking," Aristotle comments, "and they have this advantage that, while it is difficult to find similar things that have really happened in the past, it is easier to invent fables"—although he concedes that factual anecdotes are more convincing because they carry the weight of truth. Martin Luther King's "Letter From the Birmingham City Jail" contains an excellent hypothetical anecdote, about an African-American father seeing his daughter cry when he tells her why they can't visit a white-only amusement park.

Just as important as logical techniques for advancing your own argument are those for refuting opposing arguments. One can attack alternative arguments on the grounds of feasibility: I did when insisting that making the University of Maryland or Prince George's County responsible for added bus service to the university wouldn't work because of their limited resources for such a project. One can also argue that another plan doesn't apply to the problem at hand. This was my reasoning in arguing against the comparison of Prince George's County's bus system to Montgomery County's when Montgomery County's wealthier population enabled it to finance a much more extensive bus service than its less flush neighbor could. Adopting a slightly different strategy, one can protest that an opposing plan isn't necessary—that it really misses the mark of alleviating the problem. If an opposing argument actually does work, does apply to the problem, and can solve it, one could counter it on the grounds that it simply works less effectively than one's own. Most importantly, when dealing with actual opposing arguments rather than possible or hypothetical ones, look for and expose any factual or logical errors by your opponent. The methods above all involve dismissing the effect of the opposing proposal if implemented, but undermining the structure of the proposal itself casts doubt on the possibility of implementing it at all.

At the same time, guard your own argument against similar errors; aside from the obvious precaution of fact-checking, make your argument as logically air-tight as you can and be sure you can explain any apparent logical inconsistencies. Ask yourself the questions *The New St. Martin's Handbook* asks would-be proposal writers: "Do any sources contradict each other? If so, can you account for or resolve the contradictions?" And don't fool yourself into believing that you can disguise the logical flimsiness of a claim from your readers. Unlike oratory, writing excludes much of the author's personality, especially those elements—appearance, demeanor, tone and timbre of voice—that can most affect the audience's reception of the words and also distract the audience from their sense. The argument itself stands bare before the reader, even if the writer tries to dress it in the emperor's new clothes. Michael Stephens, my memoir workshop professor in graduate school at Emerson College, once said, "Writing is the worst place in the world to hide."

A key ingredient in protecting yourself from errors in reasoning and finding them in your opponents' arguments is awareness of the most common logical fallacies in persuasive writing. In circular reasoning, probably the most clearly detectable fallacy, the writer presents the cause of something as merely a rephrasing of the effect, as in Bell's illustration: "He enjoyed mountain climbing because he found pleasure in scaling large natural formations." This pseudo-explanation merely begs another question: Why does he find pleasure in scaling large natural formations? It fails to uncover the root of the reason, whether it is physical exertion, love of nature, a feeling of accomplishment, the sense of danger, or a combination of these. Lacking valid rhetorical ammunition to attack an opponent, many bad persuasive writers and speakers resort to the *ad hominem* (Latin: "to the man") fallacy, attacking aspects of the opponent himself or herself on irrelevant grounds instead of his or her argument. When John C. Fremont ran for president as the Republican Party's first nominee in 1856, opponents tried to discredit him by pointing out his illegitimate birth, when that condition did not render his platform unsound or himself incapable of running the country. It wasn't his fault, after all. Aristotle identifies the fallacy of confusing a genus with its species: "… not every rascal is a thief although every thief is a rascal."

Lunsford and Connors compile a list of other fallacies, beginning with *post hoc, ergo propter hoc* ("after this, therefore because of this")—the assumption that something occurring after a certain event must be caused by that event. The fact that you forgot to zip up your fly the first day you wore your most recently purchased pair of pants might have no bearing whatsoever on whether you will continue to leave your fly open every time you wear a new pair of pants in the future; oversleeping and rushing through dressing yourself to arrive at work on time may have caused that lapse. Next comes *non sequitur* ("it doesn't follow"), a more familiar term, which is baldly claiming that one thing results from another when no causal relationship can be demonstrated. If I were to say that because my car is in the shop I forgot to zip the fly of my pants today, I would be guilty of a *non sequitur*. The either-or fallacy preconceives that only two sides of an issue may exist when there may in actuality be more. Hasty generalization and oversimplification paint complex issues in broad strokes, ignoring significant nuances and details.

Lunsford and Connors also present "emotional fallacies" to avoid, but I don't see eye-to-eye with them on some. I agree with them on the weakness of flattery in making one's point. As in cover letters, cozying up to your audience in writing sidesteps your purpose; your audience already has a good opinion of itself, and you will be no more likely to convince it of your argument because you have a good opinion of it too. Like Lunsford and Connors, I also find veiled threats an emotional fallacy. In my bus proposal I cited a report that found lack of adequate public transportation to potential jobs to be an important factor in the Watts riots of 1965 in Los Angeles. However, I immediately clarified that I wasn't claiming that riots would erupt over bus service to the University of Maryland—merely that correcting the current inadequacy could combat socioeconomic malaise in the similar predominantly African-American and low-income area where many university employees lived. On the other hand, Lunsford and Connors categorically dismiss bandwagon appeal ("Everybody else is doing it") and in-crowd appeal ("All the cool kids are doing it"). Generally these are not serious means of persuasion, but they can be appropriate and useful in writing for business: no company wants to appear behind the times, and every company wants to appear on the cutting edge. Also, I have no idea why they mention false analogies as an emotional fallacy. If analogies don't work, that's a fallacy of logic.

We're more likely to believe arguments by writers who seem trustworthy and authoritative; this is where ethos, how the writer projects his or her character in writing, comes in. Aristotle says in the *Rhetoric*, "The orator persuades by moral character when his speech is delivered in such a manner as to render him worthy of confidence; for we feel confidence in a greater degree and more readily in persons of worth in regard to everything in general."

Ideally, Aristotle continues, "this confidence must be due to the speech itself, not to any preconceived idea of the speaker's character." Yes, a writer should establish his or her ethos in the writing itself. But if a writer has a record of and a reputation for insightful arguments on this topic or similar ones, this prior work cannot help but color our perception of his or her credibility. When the late William F. Buckley advocated drug legalization, most people took his opinion more seriously than that of Chris Robinson, lead singer of the Black Crowes, when he advocated legalizing marijuana (a position he has long since publicly recanted). William F. Buckley was the pre-eminent political commentator of his day; Chris Robinson is a rock star who has precious little else to say about the state of American society. One can weave one's credentials or experience into one's writing, as I do when referring to my proposal to increase local bus service to the University of Maryland in this article. Mentioning it too often or too elaborately, though, can backfire, making you appear conceited.

How, then, should your writing itself convey your character in a way your audience will find positive? Start by knowing as much about your audience as possible. If you can pinpoint your specific audience, you'll be more able to determine their attitudes and make yourself and your argument amenable to them. For the proposal I wrote in my Advanced Composition class in college our instructor told us to pick the one person or body of people most able to put our proposal into action. I chose Bob Sauer, who oversaw operation of all Metrobus routes in Maryland.

The New St. Martin's Handbook contains several questions about your audience whose answers you should know when writing your proposal:

"What assumptions can you make about your audience?"
"What is your audience's stance toward your topic?"
"What is your relationship to the audience?"
"What is your attitude toward your audience?"
"What attitudes will the audience expect you to hold? What attitudes might disturb or offend them?"

If you proposed sponsoring a course of gun safety classes to the NRA, you would want to focus on the responsibility that ownership and proper use of firearms entails, which bespeaks pride in a citizen's right to bear arms, rather than dwelling on the damage and death that their uncontrolled use can bring.

"In general," Lunsford and Connors continue,

writers can establish credibility in three ways:

1. by demonstrating knowledge about the topic at hand
2. by establishing common ground with the audience in the form of respect for their points of view and concern for their welfare
3. by demonstrating fairness and evenhandedness.

Logos contributes to ethos: to help convey your character as believable, show that you know what you're talking about. For all of William F. Buckley's renown, his arguments for drug legalization earned serious consideration because he employed reason and knowledge of American politics and government. Chris Robinson's argument didn't use much of anything besides drugs themselves, which probably explains why he reversed his opinion after getting clean. Ethos can improve how well-disposed your readers will be to your argument, but ethos itself will not convince them; logos still reigns supreme.

Related to Lunsford and Connors's second point above, *NTC's Business Writer's Handbook* says, "Finally, persuasion depends upon the writer's or speaker's point of view. If that point of view is 'I'-centered (that is, egotistical or self-concerned), the audience may be unwilling to accept the ideas and attitudes offered. If, on the other hand, the point of view focuses on the audience's needs and interests in a 'you'-centered way, persuasion is much more likely." Although as a student I depended on Metrobus to get home at night after the university shuttle bus stopped running, and as a campus employee I depended on it to get to and from work in the summer when the shuttle didn't run, I left that out of my college bus proposal. I kept the spotlight off of myself and on larger trends that Metro would find significant. A complimentary closing to your proposal in which you offer to work together with your audience to implement and, if needed, modify your proposal also goes a long way toward building rapport with your audience. You can demonstrate fairness and evenhandedness by acknowledging valid points in rival arguments and weak points in your own, while still trying to downplay the significance of the latter.

Establishing ethos can present a challenge when you have reason to believe your audience will not like your proposal. "If you are dealing with a reluctant, even hostile audience, you'll need a thoughtful approach," declare Diana Roberts Wienbroer et al. in *Rules of Thumb for Business Writers*. "In writing to persuade, it is particularly important that you use an inviting (that is, not alienating) tone of voice. It is possible to argue your point of view without offending others. You can be both polite and strong at the same time." "Argument" is only a technical term. Even if your audience would be naturally unfavorable toward your argument, you shouldn't make your proposal a confrontation.

Wienbroer et al. advise, "It may be more effective to come at the subject softly or indirectly." Some ways they suggest to launch into your argument obliquely are to begin with a story, an analogy, a question, or a startling statement. A master of this bait-and-switch technique was the early 20th Century British writer G. K. Chesterton, who used it in his essays to draw readers into his unpopular views as an economic radical and a Roman Catholic in Protestant England. His essays appear to be about one thing at their beginning and then, after developing this idea somewhat, he shifts its focus entirely to something incidentally connected to it. One opens with his facetious personal quest to find the greatest idiot he can; in the essay's second half, we learn that the specimen Chesterton devotes the essay to earns this title because he favors mine owners over striking miners in a labor dispute at the time.

Pathos, the emotional dimension of your argument, is the least important element of the rhetorical triangle—but still important. The problem you intend to remedy has negative effects and may have more dire consequences if left unchecked, and solving it will bring benefits; tap into the audience's fear of damage to its vital interests and desire for success. Just don't exaggerate the role of emotion in what will, after all, be a calculated professional decision. Like ethos, pathos should assist logic rather than outdoing or replacing it.

"For pathos, use description and concrete language. Also figurative language: metaphors, similes, analogies," write Lunsford and Connors. Sharp, specific, and colorful word choice packs an emotional punch. Martin Luther King uses such language in the passage in "Letter From the Birmingham City Jail" about tears filling the eyes of an African-American girl when her father tells her that an amusement park she wants to visit won't admit them, although arguably Dr. King lays it on a bit thick. Lunsford and Connors's analogy example of comparing college students in their course registration process to experimental rats trying to find their way through a maze powerfully carries the frustration, hopelessness, and depersonalization one would feel going through a convoluted bureaucratic procedure. Anecdotes also build pathos: the story of Bennie Pender's inconvenient commute to campus in my bus proposal leads the reader to empathize with his daily struggle in as simple a task as traveling to his place of employment.

The *Rhetoric* discusses a particular aspect of pathos that, while originally framed in terms of legal arguments, also applies in business: "If the speaker then … proves that those who claim our pity (and the reasons why they do so) are unworthy to obtain it and deserve that it should be refused them, then pity will be impossible." Business decisions involving an outside party and depending on evaluating that party's conduct often carry an emotional undercurrent. If a company or firm that wants to merge or partner with yours, or that your company insures, or that your company or client invests in has operated recklessly or foolishly, your report could appeal to feelings of betrayal, disappointment, and exploitation in recommending to deny assistance to that company. Likewise, if a borrower in default of a loan or a debtor overdue on payment has made little effort toward or given little guarantee of meeting his or her obligation, or if an organization or department fails quality control and has made few steps toward meeting compliance, your report will depict their behavior as cases of bad faith. If, however, the other party's setbacks were due to accidental oversight or unforeseen or uncontrollable circumstances, you may argue in the spirit of compassion to honor the other party's honest efforts. In this way, pathos in professional writing appeals to a moral dimension—it persuades the audience to give the parties in question their just deserts.

§

In contrast to the simple, lean style of expository professional writing, persuasive writing should use a vivid, energetic style. To persuade you must engage your audience, and to engage your audience it must enjoy reading what you have written. Therefore, vary the length and structure of your sentences and paragraphs to avoid monotony and to create a dynamic prose rhythm. Organizing and expressing your ideas in a variety of ways also signifies mental sophistication, which will show that your ideas themselves are probably equally sophisticated and worth entertaining, thus feeding into building ethos.

Another facet of style tied to ethos is showing consideration for your audience in your word choice. "All writers need to pay very careful attention to the ways in which their writing can either invite readers to participate as part of the audience or leave them out," says *The New St. Martin's Handbook*. "Look at the following sentence:

> As every schoolchild knows, the world is losing its rain forests at the rate of one acre per second."

While you expect your audience to hold some knowledge about your topic, don't snobbishly imply that a piece of information that you didn't learn in grade school is prerequisite for admittance to the "in crowd" of your subject matter as in the sentence above. You can't assume what or how much your audience knows; if they knew everything you know, the problem likely wouldn't exist in the first place. Don't tilt your nose in the air just because you know it yourself.

Most of all, your writing shouldn't exclude or discriminate against particular groups, regardless of whether or not they are part of your audience. Lunsford and Connors caution, "For example, a student whose paper for a religion seminar uses *we* to refer to Christians and *they* to refer to members of other religions had better be sure that all the class members and the instructor are Christian …" Even if they are Christian, the more fair-minded among them may not appreciate the writer's exclusivist tone and the implication that all of his or her readers should be Christians. Think deeply about this aspect of your writing; often we express such attitudes without knowing it. "Sometimes assumptions are so deeply ingrained that they have the effect of completely ignoring or 'erasing' large groups of people," Lunsford and Connors elaborate, "as students at the University of Kansas realized when they discovered that history books routinely reported only one survivor of General George Custer's Battle of Little Bighorn: Comanche, a horse…. Several thousand Sioux survived that battle, yet the history books simply ignored them." An area of special concern is using non-sexist terms. I make sure to use personal pronouns and adjectives to both genders in my writing: "he or she," "him or her," "his or her(s)." The instructor of my Advanced Composition course in college made a point of discussing non-sexist alternatives for traditionally male-associated terms:

humankind or *humanity*	instead of	*mankind*
human resources or *personnel*	instead of	*manpower*
chairperson or (if applicable) *chairwoman*	instead of	*chairman*
letter carrier	instead of	*mailman*
trash collector	instead of	*garbage man*

And if you use "sanitation technician" instead of either of those last terms, you should never be allowed to write again.

§

About a year after I submitted my proposal for increasing Metrobus service to the University of Maryland, another bus did start running through campus, basically along the lines of my plan. I honestly have no idea if my proposal had anything to do with that decision; I was too relieved to be finished with the immense amount of work that went into researching and writing the proposal to follow up on it after the semester ended. I contented myself with the A I received in the course. But since Bob Sauer, my audience, allowed me to interview him for the proposal and gave me printed information about Metrobus routes in Maryland, it seems likely that he had an open mind on the issue and was genuinely interested in what I had to say. Maybe my proposal just opened Metro's eyes to the university community's feelings on the issue, and they reached the same conclusions I did from their own independent investigation. Yet if Metro had chosen a different idea, or even had decided not to change, my proposal still might have succeeded. If it can make its reader stop, think, and reconsider—if it makes him or her believe that "That's the way things are" isn't a good enough reason to do something the way it's done—a proposal will have accomplished something, even if that something is less than you had hoped for.

AFTERWORD

I'd like the professional reader to take away two main ideas about writing from this book that lie latent in much of it but are rarely expressed outright. Divergent or even paradoxical as they may seem, they represent the most essential truths to keep in mind when approaching a writing project.

First, language conveys information as definitively as numbers, and using language poorly—even in conjunction with numeric data—results in information as wrong as that conveyed by incorrect numbers. Let's say your company conducted a survey, and for a particular multiple-choice question the top answer was chosen by 47% of respondents. You cannot write, "A majority of respondents selected Answer X"; by definition, a majority must equal more than half. You need to write something like "Answer X was the most prevalent response among participants" or "More respondents chose Answer X than any other answer given." Likewise, you cannot describe 24% as one-quarter or one in four. You can describe it as "roughly," "approximately," "about," "nearly," or "just under" one-quarter or one in four.

Even incidental text like that included with graphs requires care in word choice. If the data illustrated by the graph is drawn from a subset of subjects (only those for whom certain conditions apply or only those who responded to a certain previous question on surveys), indicate this clearly in your graph heading or axis labels so the reader understands that the base of the data shown isn't simply the total sample.

The errors described above aren't matters of semantics or taste—they are inaccurate data, and you and/or your company would be reporting false information if they appeared in a document you gave to your superiors or a client. Including the correct numeric data along with them might exacerbate the problem instead of fixing it: if your reader doesn't interpret the text's discrepancy from the numbers as an attempt to pull a fast one by "spinning" the data, he or she will probably take it to mean you're an idiot. Errors in spelling, punctuation, grammar, and sentence structure like those mentioned in the chapters on those topics that could alter a sentence's meaning would incur the same damage.

Despite the precision with which we must apply words in professional writing, the process of arranging them in the best order is far from cut-and-dried. Fluidity typifies the writing process. I, and most authors on writing, isolate the elements and stages of writing from one another to discuss them, but they interrelate to a great extent. "Researchers often describe the process of writing as recursive, meaning that its goals or parts are constantly flowing into and influencing one another, without any clear break among them," write Angela Lunsford and Robert Connors in *The New St. Martin's Handbook*. The rhetorical concern for ethos—for winning the reader's respect and goodwill through the writer's self-presentation—will affect the writer's voice and tone, which will in turn play a large part in what words the writer chooses. In revision, often corrections to punctuation cause changes in sentence structure, and varying or improving sentence structure usually necessitates changes in punctuation.

Don't be afraid to foray into an aspect of writing other than the one you happen to focus on at the moment in instances where they connect. Just don't get so carried away that you skip from aspect to aspect without addressing any of them thoroughly, derailing your systematic progress through a draft. Think of the elements of writing and the sequence in which you concentrate on them as a pattern to vary from and return to. Too rigorous a commitment to addressing one aspect at a time could cause you to ignore problems in other areas that you might stumble upon, or to forget them if you postpone working on them; too lax, and the composition process would devolve into chaos.

The lack of a magic formula for good writing further complicates the process. In *The Elements of Style*, William Strunk and E. B. White wonder in print,

> Who can confidently say what ignites a certain combination of words, causing them to explode in the mind?... There is no satisfactory explanation of style, no infallible guide to good writing ... no key that unlocks the door, no infallible rule by which writers may shape their course. Writers will often find themselves steering by stars that are disturbingly in motion.

Strunk and White's guidelines about writing, my guidelines about writing, and anyone else's guidelines about writing cannot be applied universally to any imaginable situation; what "rules" there are for the most appropriate choice to make in writing are determined by the nature of each writing situation. As I mentioned back in the grammar chapter, writing rules can only describe, not prescribe: they only present to the writer what tends to work best most often. It remains for the writer to decide—based on experience, intuition sharpened by experience, and sensitivity to the circumstances of the writing's context—whether a work of writing fits into a certain rule or is an exception to it.

Moreover, guidelines about different considerations sometimes clash: the writer must weigh the competing considerations and give the most important one in that situation priority. The term "score" for the number twenty had already become antiquated, if not obsolete, by the time Abraham Lincoln penned the Gettysburg Address. For any other occasion, the president should have begun the speech, "Eighty-seven years ago ..." By instead choosing the phrase "Fourscore and seven years ago," Lincoln imbued his homage to the soldiers who sacrificed themselves to preserve the Union with the solemn, august tone of the King James Bible (Psalms 90:10: "The days of our years are threescore years and ten ...") and made its opening sentence one of the most famous and memorable lines of prose ever written in our language. President Lincoln prioritized appropriate tone over standard diction. The soldiers' lofty self-sacrifice for a greater good warranted diction equally lofty; ordinary word choice would not have sufficed to praise their extraordinary deeds. "The fact that a word or phrase satisfies one set of criteria is no guarantee that it satisfies all," British novelist Kingsley Amis writes in *The King's English*. "And not only that, either. If a sentence keeps all the rules you know and still seems wrong, change it. That takes longer, but so does anything worthwhile."

This is what makes writing an art, not a science. The writer can know how to get where he or she needs to go only by starting the journey. Yet for all this procedural uncertainty, the writer needs dexterity with his or her peculiar tools to achieve his or her goal—just as a painter must have a grasp of perspective, form, color, and so on to execute his or her vision effectively, although that vision might not fully define itself until he or she has started painting. The more journeys the writer takes, the more of a feel the writer acquires for the tools of grammar, spelling, diction (as demonstrated in this chapter's first section), syntax, structure, and rhetoric, the more likely he or she will figure out how to use them to successfully arrive at the end of the next journey.

Get writing!

BIBLIOGRAPHY

Amis, Kingsley. *The King's English: A Guide to Modern Usage*. New York: St. Martin's, 1998

Aristotle. *"Art" of Rhetoric*. Trans. John Henry Freese. Loeb Classic Library. Cambridge: Harvard University Press, 1982.

Bell, Arthur H. *NTC's Business Writer's Handbook*. Lincolnwood: NTC, 1996.

Bryson, Bill. *Bryson's Dictionary of Troublesome Words: A Writer's Guide to Getting It Right*. New York: Random House, 2002.

Degen, Michael. *Crafting Expository Argument*. Garland: Telemachos Publishing, 2000.

Lunsford, Andrea and Robert Connors. *The New St. Martin's Handbook*. Boston: Bedford/St. Martin's, 1999.

Strunk, William Jr. and E. B. White. *The Elements of Style*. New York: Longman, 2000. 4th Ed.

The American Heritage Dictionary of the English Language, 4th Ed. Boston: Houghton Mifflin, 2000.

Truss, Lynne. *Eats, Shoots and Leaves*. New York: Penguin, 2004.

Wienbroer, Diana Roberts, Elaine Hughes, and Jay Silverman. *Rules of Thumb For Business Writers*. New York: McGraw-Hill, 2000.